THINGS IN THE BASEMENT

I0430227

A History of Halloween Horrors

By John Lloyd Retzer

For My Father,

John G. Retzer,

Who Introduced Me To The Works Of

Ray Bradbury:

The October Country, The Halloween Tree, Something Wicked This Way Comes, A Medicine For Melancholy and more

And For My Mother,

Gloria D. Retzer

Who Spent Far Too Many Hours Sewing Halloween Costumes To Make The Holiday Special For Her Boys

Table of Contents

Introduction 7

Halloween's Origins 8

Trick-or-Treating 21

Halloween Around The World 26

Aliens 30

Black Cats, Ravens and Other Familiars 39

Devils 47

Fortune Telling 53

Frankenstein's Monster 59

Ghosts 65

Ghouls 73

Goblins 76

Headless Horsemen 80

The Jack O'Lantern 84

Mad Scientists 88

Mad Slashers and Psychos 95

The Men In Black 104

The Mummy 107

Robots 113

Scarecrows 118

Skeletons 123

Vampires	127
Werewolves	142
Witches	153
Zombies	162
Postscript	172
About This Book	174
Thanks	176
About The Author	177

BY THE PRICKING OF MY THUMBS,

SOMETHING WICKED THIS WAY COMES

MACBETH ACT IV SCENE 1

Introduction

Halloween is my favorite holiday. In this, I am not alone. Marketing studies show that seventy percent of Americans celebrate the occasion in some fashion. Overall, it is the third most popular Holiday, behind Christmas and Thanksgiving. In 2011, Americans collectively spent nearly $7 billion on costumes, candy and decorations. And if Halloween reflects a general American love of horror tropes, with all the books, movies and games, the total moves to the tens of billions. The "zombie industry" alone generated some $6 billion in 2011.

In many ways, Halloween is the quintessential American Holiday. Halloween's traditions, activities, imagery and stories are -- like American culture in general -- a mishmash of ideas from across the world, brought here by successive waves of immigrants. Add to those a little homegrown American inventiveness and creativity and therein lies the modern Halloween celebration.

Things In The Basement: A History of Halloween Horrors is a exploration of Halloween's origins and of the horrors that keep us up at night.

Halloween's Origins

Each year on Halloween night, millions of children take to the streets in scary costumes to beg for treats at the doors of their neighbors. At the same time, millions of adults enjoy the holiday as a celebration of things that go bump in the night, and frighten the unwary.

Few, however, ever stop to wonder about the origins of the night, or of the creatures that seem to populate it.

Most sources trace Halloween's origins to an ancient Celtic holiday called Samhain. The Celts were a group of people who lived in present day Ireland and England from about the 5th Century B.C. An agricultural people, the Celts (as did many ancients) marked the equinoxes as major events.

Samhain (pronounced sow-en) was an end of the summer commemoration that occurred near the end of October. Because the present day calendar was not in effect then, there is no way to know a precise date.

The end of summer was a significant event for ancient peoples because it represented the end of warmth, sunlight and times of plenty, and the entry into a time of shorter days, colder nights, and deprivation. Such dark times were thought to be accompanied by dark spirits.

It is doubtful that anyone really knows how the Celts celebrated their holiday, but several stories have emerged.

One story says that the Celts believed that on Halloween night, the spirits of the people who had died in the previous year came back to the Earth, to search for a body to occupy. To avoid being possessed, the superstitious Celts would put out all the lights of their village in an attempt to convince the spirits that no one was at home. Then, the villagers would dress in costumes designed to trick the spirits into thinking that they, too were spirits, and thus not eligible to be possessed.

If all went well, the spirits would wander through the village, and see nothing but dark houses and other spirits. They would then wander off to another village.

Michael Drayton, in his poem *Poly-Olbion* (1612), describes the Celtic druids and their practices:

> *If, as those Druids taught, which kept the British rites,*
>
> *And dwelt in darksome groves, there counselling with sprites,*
>
> *When these our souls by death our bodies do forsake*
>
> *They instantly again do other bodies take——"*

In these Celtic beliefs, are the origins of several of the modern Halloween traditions: Ghosts (spirits of the dead) costumes and dark, empty houses.

Samhain also may contain the roots of trick-or-treating. One story says that the Celts would leave on their doorsteps gifts of food and drink to appease the wandering spirits. As night ended, the villagers found that they were without lights. They then would relight all of their hearth fires from a sacred bonfire maintained by their priests, the Druids.

A more gruesome version says that part of the bonfire ceremony involved the ignition of a young, innocent village girl. This, however, is more Hollywood than history.

Another version - more pedestrian - is that the Celts celebrated their end of summer holiday with a huge bonfire. The villagers would put out their own fireplaces and gather to sacrifice crops and animals to the fire. Costumes of animals were worn to further honor the creatures that had blessed them throughout the summer's bounty. At the end, each family would relight their hearths from the sacred communal fire.

Sacred fires may also have been lit with the wheel-and-spindle friction method. The wheel was in this case a symbol of the sun, and spun east to west, would give hope of renewal in the spring.

Sacrifices of animals likely were a part of any celebration. Druids may have "read" the entrails to divine the future, likely reassuring the village of spring renewal.

The Celts were one of many peoples conquered by the Romans in the early part of the first Century. The Romans were highly adaptive, and happily adopted local holidays, gods and traditions as their own. (That is why so many Roman gods bear an uncanny resemblance to Greek ones and why the Roman Empire was later able to shift from paganism to Christianity. If there was a better idea, they stole it.).

The Romans had their own fall harvest festivals. One, for the Goddess Pomona, celebrated the harvest of the fruit of the trees. Pomona was depicted as a maiden with fruit in her arms and a pruning knife in hand. The apple was her symbol, which has led some scholar to speculate that this is the origin of the custom of bobbing for apples (Whatever the origins, illustrations in medieval manuscripts show people bobbing for apples, so the custom dates to at least then.)

Pomona's festival day was November 1, a date which generally marked the completion of the fall harvest. The happy coincidence with the Celtic Samhain made it all the easier to integrate the two.

The Romans also had their own festival of the Dead, called Feralia, which was marked at the end of the Roman year, in February.

Signs of the merger of these two traditions extend through the ages. Fruits and nuts, as well as apples, have served as Halloween treats. Several divination games popular in the former Celtic lands — England, Ireland and Scotland in particular — use fruits and nuts as fortune tellers.

Christianity was introduced to the British Isles starting about the second century A.D. Just as the Romans had been willing to adapt to local customs, so were the early Christian missionaries — many of whom were Roman. Midsummer was dedicated to the birth of St. John. Lugnasad became Lammas, and it is thought that the date of Christmas was selected to coincide with a Germanic winter festival.

When the inhabitants of England and Ireland proved unwilling to abandon their late October festival, Christianity simply incorporated it.

On May 13, 609 Pope Boniface IV consecrated Rome's pagan Pantheon in the name of early Christian martyrs. The day was to honor these as "Saints" for their beliefs — thus, "Saint's Day." Later, Pope Gregory III reworked the calendar to designate November 1 as All Saints Day — a day to honor Saints and Martyrs. The day was also known as All Hallows, and the previous night, All Hallows Eve. November 2 was named All Souls Day, and was set aside to honor the souls of the dead. The three days together were called Hallow Mass.

All Hallows Eve, of course, was later corrupted into Halloween.

It is widely believed that Boniface IV did this to co-opt the pagan Celtic holdouts into Christianity.

Fires that once were built for sacrifices and to bring back the sun of spring now ere lit to protect against Satan. Costumes to ward off the spirits were incorporated into masquerades for the saints. Food left to appease the wandering dead was renamed "soul cakes" and used to honor the deceased. Petitions to the pagan Lords of Death became prayers for the souls of deceased family and friends.

By the 12th Century, Hallow Mass practices had spread throughout Europe. Church bells were rung in villages, and people visited graveyards to light candles and leave offerings.

With the rise of Protestant power in England —
and especially during the reign of Cromwell and the
Puritans — traditional Catholic holidays came
under attack. Cromwell, after all, even banned
Christmas celebrations. Hallowmas suffered
accordingly, and increasingly was supplanted by
Guy Fawkes Night. The tradition remained strong,
however, in Ireland and in Scotland.

Hallow Mass traditions of souling are mentioned
in John Brand's *Observations on Popular Antiquities of
Great Britain*:

> On Allhallows Day or Hallowmass, it was an
> ancient English custom for poor persons and
> beggars to go a-souling, which signified to go
> round asking for money, to fast for the souls of
> the donors of alms or their kins-folk.

Scottish poet Robert Burns wrote a paean to
Halloween in 1785, revealing the extent to which the
holiday had become embedded in that culture.
Guising, in which children disguised in costume
went from door to door for treats with scooped out
turnips was first recorded in Scotland in the 19th
century.

Halloween arrived in North America with the early colonists. However, because of the Puritan influence in New England, it was mostly confined to the Scots-Irish of the Southern Colonies. Puritan colonials followed the lead of their brethren in England, and purged their calendar of all the Catholic "Saint's Days." Puritan New England recognized only Muster Day, Election Day, Harvard Commencement and later, Thanksgiving. Guy Fawkes Day, with its inherent anti-Catholic sentiments likely also survived.

The diary of Samuel Sewall, a Puritan Judge, notes one such Guy Fawkes Day celebration:

Wednesday, Novf 4'.!' The County Court was Adjourned to Thorsday come Senight at 2 aclock.

Mr. Allin preached Novy 5. 1G85 — finished his Text 1 Jn? 1. 9. mentioned not a word in Prayer or Preaching that I took notice of with respect to Gun-powder Treason. Part of the 132'^ Ps. sung; viz. from 11"/ v. The Lord to David Sware — to the End. In the Even I met at Serj! Bull's with Capt. Frary, Serj'^ Gardener, Pell, Raynsford, Corp'l Odlin, Quinsey, Paddy, Clerk Mason, Wheeler ; Ten mentioned sate down to Super, Serj* Bull and his Wife waited : After by the Fire spake as to an Ensign, all said they were unanimous for Serj* Gardener upon Serjl^ Bull's refusal, who alledged, as formerly, the loss of 's 4t!' Finuer of 's ri<»:lit Hand, and a Pain in the

*same Shoulder : and as to me, is not of any
Church, nor a Freeman, nor of Estate, besides the
former Objections. Altliough it rained hard, yet
there was a Bonfire made on the Coinon, about 50
attended it.*

*Friday night being fair about two hundred
hallowed about a Fire on the Coinon.*

Pagan bonfire traditions, then, survived in Puritan New England.

Elsewhere, colonial "Halloweens" (if they even were called that) were essentially Harvest Festivals, with lots of eating and drinking, music, dancing, ghost stories and fortune telling (it not hard to see why it did not catch on with the Puritans). Some more of our modern Halloween symbols were introduced at this time, as traditions were blended with Native American harvest festivals. Corn stalks and pumpkins - unknown in Europe before the discovery of North America - became part of Halloween imagery.

Even if Halloween was not celebrated specifically, the spirit world still was a part of colonial lives. The infamous Salem Witch Trials of 1692 were steeped in the occult. Colonials consulted fortune tellers, employed good luck charms and hex signs, and feared the handiwork of the devil.

Halloween really arrived in America with the massive Irish immigration of the 1840s. The Irish brought their Halloween traditions and wove them into the fabric of American society.

Still, Halloween itself seems not to be "officially" recognized in the United States until early 1900s at the very least. The "United States Almanac for the Year of Our Lord 1840" lists All Saints Day (Nov 1.) and All Souls Day (Nov. 2), but nothing on October 31. It also is missing from the Connecticut Almanac of 1897, the Times Almanac of 1889, and the American Almanac and Repository of Useful Knowledge of 1900. Halloween's first appearance in the Chicago Daily News Almanac is in 1911.

Halloween themed postcards date to the late 1800s, so the celebrations undoubtedly occurred prior to a wider, or "official," acceptance of the holiday. In her 1919 history titled "The Book of Hallowe'en" historian Ruth Edna Kelley writes that at that time:

> *Hallowe'en parties are the real survival of the ancient merrymakings. They are prepared for in secret. Guests are not to divulge the fact that they are invited. Often they come masked, as ghosts or witches.*

> *The decorations make plain the two elements of the festival. For the centerpiece of the table there may be a hollowed pumpkin, filled with apples and nuts and other fruits of harvest, or a*

pumpkin-chariot drawn by field-mice. So it is clear that this is a harvest-party, like Pomona's feast. In the coach rides a witch, representing the other element, of magic and prophecy. Jack-o'-lanterns, with which the room is lighted, are hollowed pumpkins with candles inside. The candle-light shines through holes cut like features. So the lantern becomes a bogy, and is held up at a window to frighten those inside. Corn-stalks from the garden stand in clumps about the room. A frieze of witches on broomsticks, with cats, bats, and owls surmounts the fireplace, perhaps. A full moon shines over all, and a caldron on a tripod holds fortunes tied in nut-shells. The prevailing colors are yellow and black: a deep yellow is the color of most ripe grain and fruit; black stands for black magic and demoniac influence. Ghosts and skulls and cross-bones, symbols of death, startle the beholder. Since Hallowe'en is a time for lovers to learn their fate, hearts and other sentimental tokens are used to good effect, as the Scotch lads of Burns's time wore love-knots.

Having marched to the dining-room to the time of a dirge, the guests find before them plain, hearty fare; doughnuts, gingerbread, cider, popcorn, apples, and nuts honored by time. The Hallowe'en cake has held the place of honor since

*the beginning here in America. A ring, key,
thimble, penny, and button baked in it foretell
respectively speedy marriage, a journey,
spinsterhood, wealth, and bachelorhood.*

Such traditions do not spring up overnight, and probably had been going on for many years.

From the 1920s to the late 1940s, Halloween seems to have developed a bad reputation. While minor tricks always had been a part of the tradition, the tricks had turned to vandalism that seriously damaged property and threatened public safety. In 1934, the Oregon Journal reported in an article with the headline: *Halloween Pranks Keep Police On Hop* that:

> *"Other young goblins and ghosts, employing
> modern shakedown methods, successfully worked
> the 'trick or treat' system in all parts of the city."*

The misbehavior perhaps peaked with Detroit's "Devil's Night" rampages of arson and vandalism, which began in the early 1940s and continue to this day.

Adults were not pleased with the direction of the holiday, often comparing it to extortion and a "shake down racket." Halloween violence resulted in the holiday being banned in some communities. Others fought back by organizing Halloween parties and parades.

Community Halloween activities seem to have been born in Anoka, Minnesota, the self-proclaimed "Halloween Capital of the World." The town's parade and carnival were started in 1920 as an effort to stop destructive Halloween pranks. The festival has been held every year with the exception of 1942 and 1943.

It was the Baby Boomers who put Halloween front and center in American society. Halloween and trick-or-treating made an appearance in Jack and Jill magazine in 1947. It also appeared on several radio shows, including Ozzie and Harriet in the late 1940s. An October 1951 Peanuts comic shows the characters in costume presumably off to either a party or trick-or-treating. UNICEF conducted its first national Halloween fundraising campaign in 1953.

Today, Halloween ranks second only to Christmas as a retail event. In 2011, Americans spent nearly $7 billion on the holiday. Costumes accounted for $2.5 billion of the total. Another $2 billion was spent on candy, and a similar amount for decorations. More than six hundred million pounds of candy was purchased in 2011.

Trick-or-Treating

At its core, trick-or-treating echoes elements of the ancient Celtic Samhain celebration. At summer's end, when the dead were said to walk the Earth, food and drink was set on doorsteps to appease the returning spirits. Frightened pagans dressed as spirits and demons to trick the dead and avoid possession.

As the holiday was Christianized in the 700s, villagers were encouraged to merge their pagan traditions into new ones. Christian Celts were encouraged to offer "soul cakes" for church blessings, rather than food and drink to satisfy spirits. Masquerade parades were held in which the faithful dressed as saints rather than demons. Bonfires were set to honor Christian traditions instead of pagan.

From that grew the medieval practice of Souling. Medieval theology held that when a person died, they would go to Heaven if they lead a good life, to Hell if they did not, and to Purgatory if they were somewhere in between. A family could get the souls of their loved ones out of Purgatory and into Heaven if enough prayers were offered.

On Hallow Mass, beggars would take advantage of this belief by wandering from house to house offering to say prayers in exchange for food. The "soul cakes" baked in lieu of pagan spirit offerings often were distributed.

A similar tradition, called wassailing, is associated with Christmas.

Among the earliest literary references to the practice of begging at Halloween comes from Shakespeare in "Two Gentlemen of Verona" (1593).:

> *to watch like one that fears robbing; to*
>
> *speak puling, like a beggar at Hallowmas.*

In 1777, John Brand wrote in *Observations on Popular Antiquities of Great Britain* that:

> *On Allhallows Day or Hallowmass, it was an ancient English custom for poor persons and beggars to go a-souling, which signified to go round asking for money, to fast for the souls of the donors of alms or their kins-folk.*

In Scotland, trick-or-treating was called "guising." Dating back to at least 1895, guising involved costumed participants, carrying turnip jack-o-lanterns, who roamed from door to door seeking treats.

In these customs, we have the origins of the modern Halloween custom of "Trick-or-Treating." Indeed, among many older people, trick-or-treaters still are known as "beggars."

As with so many things, immigrants to the New World brought their traditions. Scotch-Irish settlers continued their harvest celebrations in the American colonies and later in the new United States with various harvest festivals and parties. These generally included food, drink, costumes, fortune telling, ghost stories and often parades.

Prints from the late 19th and early 20th centuries — especially postcards — show many children in costume, but none apparently show children at doors. Halloween in those days was apparently celebrated mostly in parties. This supports Ruth Edna Kelley's statement in her 1919 volume, The Book of Hallowe'en, that *"Hallowe'en parties are the real survival of the ancient merrymakings"*

The first modern references to Trick Or Treating are from newspapers in the early 1900s. Unfortunately, the Halloween night activities of youth often were accompanied by violence, arson and vandalism.

In 1927, the phrase "trick-or-treating" appeared in an Alberta, Canada newspaper article. In it, the reporter noted a series of pranks, including stolen wagon wheels, gates and barrels. The pranksters demanded "edible plunder by the word trick or treat to which the inmates (of the homes) gladly responded and sent the robbers away rejoicing."

Children's costume parades once again became popular in the 1920s, and continued through the 1940s. By the 1950s, with the baby boom and the development of suburban communities, the practice of trick-or-treating was once again in full swing.

Trick or Treating — or a derivative — is practiced in several countries, including the United States, Canada, the United Kingdom, Ireland, France Puerto Rico and parts of Mexico.

The Mexican version is called calaverita (little skull) and Mexican trick-or-treaters say "can you give me my little skull." The skull in this case is a small candy made of sugar or chocolate.

In recent years, the custom of trick-or-treating has been darkened by the specter of poisoned treats. Wild media reports — even from the normally clear-headed Ann Landers — have warned of razor blades in candy bars and arsenic in pixie sticks.

Reputable studies, however, have shown that these reports are only myths. In fact, most of the urban legend can be traced back to one incident: In 1974, a father poisoned his own son with cyanide, and then attempted to cover his crime by lacing candy in the child's bag with the poison. The candy was not handed out to the neighborhood kids.

Another case occurred in 1970, when a Detroit child died of a heroin overdose that reportedly came from his Halloween candy. It turned out that he had been exposed to his uncle's drug supply.

Joel Best, a professor of Sociology at Cal State Fresno has studied U.S. newspapers published between 1958 and 1988 and found that almost all of the cases were hoaxes perpetrated by kids or misinterpretations of the facts.

Halloween Around The World

Today, Halloween celebrations with costumes, trick-or-treating and Hollywood monsters are the order of the day in the United States, Canada and Ireland.

In Mexico, it is celebrated as El Dia De Los Muertos, a three-day celebration that begins on October 31, and ends on All Souls Day. Like North America's Halloween, the event is a complex mixture of cultural traditions. It can be traced to Aztec ceremonies honoring the dead, which apparently were traditionally held in August. Spanish priests moved the event to coincide with All Souls Day, hoping to co-opt the natives into Catholicism.

Observances of the holiday apparently vary from region to region - and village to village - so it is hard to generalize, but it seems that they all observe the common practice of honoring the dead.

During this festival, the dead are supposed to return to their earthly homes on October 31, so all manner of things are set out to make them feel welcome. Some families will build a small display that includes photographs, candy, decorations, the deceased's favorite food and so on. Some will go so far as to set out wash basins and towels. On November 2, families will gather to clean up and decorate the gravesites of the departed.

More modern Mexican families apparently will skip much of this and celebrate mainly by sharing a family feast where a "Bread of the Dead" is served. Each loaf contains a small plastic toy skeleton, which is said to be good luck to the one who finds it. Families also will celebrate by giving each other gifts with a skull or skeleton theme. This is similar to the King Cake of Mardi Gras, in which a small plastic baby (said to represent the baby Jesus) is hidden in the cake.

The holiday also is often marked with a parade, in which the participants dress up as skeletons, ghosts and other ghoulish creatures, and carry a coffin through the town. Spectators will throw fruit, flowers and candies at the participants.

In England, Halloween is overshadowed by Guy Fawkes day, which is celebrated on November 5. Fawkes was a Catholic sympathizer who attempted to blow up the Parliament building and kill the protestant King James. He was caught and executed on November 5. 1605. As the story goes, after his execution, bonfires were lit in which Englishmen burned effigies of the Pope. Later, the effigies of the Pope became effigies of Fawkes himself. The event is commemorated in the Guy Fawkes Day song, first sung in the 1600s, and made famous to modern audiences with the *V For Vendetta* comics and movie.

> *Please to remember the fifth of November*
>
> *And the terrible gunpowder plot*
>
> *I can think of no reason*
>
> *Why gunpowder treason*
>
> *Ever should be forgot*

Today, Guy Fawkes Day still is celebrated in England, although the extent of the celebration varies. In some communities children will go about, carrying an effigy, or "Guy" and ask for a "penny for the Guy."

In China, Ghost Day is celebrated on the fifteenth day of the seventh lunar month. As with Samhain, on Ghost Day the spirits of the dead are said to return to the world of the living. Traditionally, offerings are made to the ancestors in the form of food, burning incense and items made from papier-mache. Fearing bad luck from disgruntled spirits, people traditionally made an effort on Ghost Day to stay indoors, particularly after dark. There also are spring and fall festivals in which the living are expected to pay their respects to the dead.

Aliens

While mankind's fear of the spirit world has perhaps faded, fear of the unknown has not. Science has replaced superstition only in offering alternative explanations for the Things In The Basement. The many aliens that now populate Halloween and horror imagery offer a variation on the science-gone-amok theme begun in works like Frankenstein and Dr Jekyll. The superior technology of the inhabitants of flying saucers is an example of how we are threatened by science, but in this case, it is a science far greater than our own.

One explanation for old horrors is that they may perhaps be nothing more than visitations by alien beings. Science fiction writer Arthur C. Clarke wrote that "any technology sufficiently advanced is indistinguishable from magic." If so, there is the possibility that many magical beings, such as ancient gods, monsters and angels were in fact aliens with fantastic technology. From this perspective, faerie abductions were alien abductions. Changelings were alien infants. Witches, vampires, werewolves and the like all are explained as close encounters of the alien kind. The effect, though, is still largely the same: Blood sucking undead are no less horrifying than blood extracting aliens.

Some folklorists believe that there is ample evidence of ancient alien visitations. In 1968, author Erich Von Daniken published *Chariots of the Gods*, in which he argued that signs of ancient visitors could be seen in ancient artwork and in monuments such as the pyramids, Stonehenge, the Moai on Easter Island and the Nazca lines in Peru. Von Daniken and others even contend that the "wheels" seen by Ezekiel were in fact, flying saucers. From the book of Ezekiel, Chapter 10:

> *9 And when I looked, behold the four wheels by the cherubim, one wheel by one cherub, and another wheel by another cherub: and the appearance of the wheels was as the colour of a beryl stone.*
>
> *10 And as for their appearances, they four had one likeness, as if a wheel had been in the midst of a wheel.*
>
> *11 When they went, they went upon their four sides; they turned not as they went, but to the place whither the head looked they followed it; they turned not as they went.*
>
> *12 And their whole body, and their backs, and their hands, and their wings, and the wheels, were full of eyes round about, even the wheels that they four had.*

13 As for the wheels, it was cried unto them in my hearing, O wheel.

14 And every one had four faces: the first face was the face of a cherub, and the second face was the face of a man, and the third the face of a lion, and the fourth the face of an eagle.

15 And the cherubim were lifted up. This is the living creature that I saw by the river of Chebar.

16 And when the cherubim went, the wheels went by them: and when the cherubim lifted up their wings to mount up from the earth, the same wheels also turned not from beside them.

17 When they stood, these stood; and when they were lifted up, these lifted up themselves also: for the spirit of the living creature was in them.

Aliens probably first became associated with Halloween thanks to Orson Welles' 1938 dramatization of H.G. Wells' *War of the Worlds*. The radio show, broadcast as a Halloween feature on October 30, was presented as a series of fictional, but realistic news bulletins. The realistic portrayal apparently confused a significant number of listeners, some of whom may have believed that an alien invasion was underway. No one knows just how many fell for Welles' theatrics (although he apparently had no intention of fooling people), but the legend of the Halloween broadcast has grown over the years.

A great deal of modern folklore has grown up around aliens and their "flying saucers." Much of the mythology centers around the Roswell Crash, several well-publicized "close encounters" and the mysterious "Men In Black."

The modern UFO "craze" may be the result of Kenneth Arnold's June 1947 sighting of several objects over Mt. Rainier while he was piloting a plane from Chehalis to Yakima, Washington. The objects, he said, skipped like saucers across a pond at speeds faster than an aircraft. Arnold reported the objects upon landing, apparently believing they were a possible Soviet threat. The story became a media sensation and from his description, the term "flying saucer" was born.

Modern UFOlogists consider Arnold's sighting the beginning of the "modern" UFO era.

Arnold's sighting was not the only incident in 1947. On July 8, Walter Haut, public information officer for Roswell Army Air Field issued a press release stating that the Army Air Force had recovered a crashed "flying disk" on a ranch near Roswell, New Mexico. The next day, Eighth Air Force commanding General Roger Ramey corrected that statement, saying the object was a balloon. A follow-up press conference showed debris that was supposed to be a weather balloon.

The story caused a stir and then was forgotten. Some thirty years later, Stanton Friedman, a physicist and "ufologist," conducted an interview with Major Jesse Marcel, who was involved with the debris recovery and was of the opinion that it was the recovery of an alien spacecraft. Given the intense interest in UFOs in the 1970s and early 1980s, the story quickly gained traction. By 1989, the story had been amended by mortician Glenn Dennis, who claimed that alien autopsies were conducted.

The incident inspired dozens of books, articles and movies. In 1995, the Air Force declassified their version of the incident, saying that it was the crash of a test of high altitude balloons designed to sniff out Soviet atomic bomb blasts. The report has not convinced UFO believers.

On January 7, 1948, Air National Guard Captain Thomas Mantell was called to pursue a flying circular object that had been spotted from a control tower at Fort Knox. Mantell had no oxygen mask, but flew past 25,000 feet trying to close with the object. At that point, he apparently lost consciousness and crashed. As with the Roswell incident, the UFO sighting was attributed to a weather balloon. The death of a military pilot in pursuit of a UFO, however, lent a sinister and menacing air to the alien story.

A wide variety of explanations have been offered for UFO sightings such as experimental military aircraft, weather balloons and satellites. Lens flares and reflections may explain their appearance in photographs. Natural phenomena such as swamp gas, ball lightning and lenticular clouds also have been named. Lenticular clouds are a particularly interesting explanation. These lens-shaped cloud, sometimes stacked, appear over mountain ranges — exactly the sort of place where many UFOs are sighted.

The notion of alien abduction was added to UFO lore with the tale of Betty and Barney Hill. On September 19, 1961, the couple spotted what they thought was a UFO while driving near Groveton, New Hampshire. They apparently spent much of the night in pursuit of the craft, stopping at several points. The object was described as like a giant pancake, and the couple claims they saw as many as a dozen figures in portholes. After that night, the couple began to experience strange sensations and disturbing dreams. The nightmares involved being "abducted" and medically examined by the short gray aliens piloting the craft.

The couple sought help, and under hypnosis further details began to emerge. In 1966, John G. Fuller published *The Interrupted Journey* about the incident. The book, written with the cooperation of the Hills and their doctor, gained international fame.

Skeptics note that Barney Hill's story and his description of the aliens resembles an episode of *The Outer Limits*, which aired just before he went into hypnotic therapy. Others say that the couple's experience were hallucinations caused by the stress of being an interracial couple when such relationships were uncommon.

Halloween aliens often are depicted as small (perhaps five feet tall) green or silvery creatures, with smooth skin, large heads, big black eyes and small noses. The grey colored versions are the aliens that the Hills claim abducted them. Other alien abduction stories have included the same basic descriptions. "Greys" are also the supposed object of the Roswell Alien autopsies.

The Hills, however, were not the first to describe the Greys. Several writers, including H.G. Wells in his *First Men In The Moon*, have described similar creatures. As noted earlier, the Hills' descriptions bear a seemingly more than coincidental similarity to a contemporary *Outer Limits* episode.

Several interesting explanations for that particular alien appearance have emerged. One is that the Greys represent in our shared imaginations a vision of the evolution of humanity. In that future, our brains continue to evolve, while our bodies atrophy from lack of physical activity.

Another theory is that the Greys actually resemble an infant's perceptions of his or her parents. A person leaning over a crib must surely appear to an infant as a creature with enormous head and eyes. It is comforting, though, because that creature offers care and comfort. That image then comes out of the deepest recesses of our memories in times of stress or under hypnosis.

Human infants themselves have small noses, and enormous heads and eyes in proportion to their bodies. Those characteristics, according to zoologist Konrad Lorenz, trigger in humans the instinct to care for the baby. The characteristic "cuteness" of babies, therefore, is a survival strategy. Once again, under stress or hypnosis, these deeply embedded feelings may emerge.

Whatever the story behind the imagery, Greys (or their green cousins) now are the dominant media version of aliens. It is not surprising, therefore, that so many current alien sightings and abduction stories involve the Greys. Given the coverage, it is now very difficult to tell whether a person reporting a grey alien sighting is describing what they actually saw, or what they expected to see.

Black Cats, Ravens and Other Familiars

Black cats, owls, ravens, toads and rats have entered Halloween lore largely by virtue of their reputations as witches' familiars. Their associations with witchcraft, however, often have deeper roots.

"Familiars" are animals (although they may also be demons in humanoid form) used by witches to assist in their magical practices. In a well-documented witchcraft trial in England in 1582, Ursula Kemp was accused of keeping four familiars: A grey cat, a black cat, a toad and a lamb. The accuser, Kemp's own eight year old son, said that she had let them suck blood from her body. Kemp had used the creatures, it was said, to make her victims ill or lame, and had even sent the familiars to kill.

Cats — most often of the black variety — are probably the most well known witches' familiars. Modern depictions of witches somehow seem incomplete without a cat lurking somewhere nearby. Indeed, cats by themselves have become powerful Halloween symbols.

Several factors contribute to cats' prominence in Halloween lore. First and foremost are the feline's nocturnal habits. In times when mankind feared the setting of the sun, creatures of the night were viewed with fear and suspicion. Cats, who so easily navigate in the dark, could easily be thought of as the servants of witches or as witches themselves.

Cat's eyes — unblinking slits that glow with reflected light — create a malevolent appearance that likely has added to their reputation as the servants of witches. The glow is characteristic of nocturnal animals, which have a reflective layer behind the retina that sends light back into the eye. The layer, the *tapetum lucidum*, enables the creatures to operate in very low light conditions.

The domestic cat's association with hearth and home also contributed to the belief in cats as familiars. As it was women who primarily were charged with witchcraft, so too did women's household implements come under suspicion. Thus, brooms, cooking pots (cauldrons) and cats became symbols of witchcraft.

Finally, the cat's wicked claws, predatory instincts and seemingly evil habit of playing with its prey only added to its reputation.

While the Kemp witchcraft trial names both black and grey, black is the archetypal color for a witch's cat. That is likely because western cultures associate black with death, disease and evil.

Interestingly, while Americans generally view black cats as bad luck, the opposite is true in other parts of the world. In Asia, Germany and parts of the United Kingdom, black cats can be good luck. Sailors sometimes kept black cats to ensure a safe voyage.

Like cats, owls likely owe their place in witchcraft and Halloween folklore to their nocturnal habits and eyes. Their fearsome claws and beaks add to the terror. The birds certainly have been noticed since ancient times. Paintings of owls are seen in prehistoric caves drawings. Greek mythology associates owls with wisdom, for they were the symbol of Athena. The Romans on the other hand, considered it a bird of "ill omen." Pliny the Elder writes:

> *The horned owl is especially funereal, and is greatly abhorred in all auspices of a public nature: it inhabits deserted places, and not only desolate spots, but those of a frightful and inaccessible nature: the monster of the night, its voice is heard, not with any tuneful note, but emitting a sort of shriek. Hence it is that it is looked upon as a direful omen to see it in a city, or even so much as in the day-time.*

In John Keats' *Hyperion*, among the "omens drear" were the "gloom-bird's hated screech."

> *For as among us mortals omens drear*

Fright and perplex, so also shuddered he-

Not at dog's howl, or gloom-bird's hated screech,

Or the familiar visiting of one

Upon the first toll of his passing-bell,

Or prophesyings of the midnight lamp;

But horrors, portion'd to a giant nerve,

Oft made Hyperion ache.

Many Native American tribes thought that owls were inhabited by spirits of the dead, a belief that found its way into frontier folklore and later to the larger American society.

The toad (or perhaps a frog) as a familiar is mentioned in Shakespeare's Macbeth

Witch 3: That will be ere the set of sun

Witch 1: Where the place

Witch 2: Upon the heath

Witch 3: There to meet with Macbeth

Witch 1: I come, Graymalkin!

Witch 2: Paddock calls – Anon!

Witch. I come, Graymalkin!

All: Fair is foul and foul is fair

Hover through the fog and filthy air

Paddock, in the passage above, is a Renaissance era term for a frog, or toad.

Toads have a lot working against them. As a whole, they are not particularly attractive creatures, who tend to live in damp, dark places — the perfect climate for evil. Glands in the toad's skin secrete toxins, which can cause a range of medical issues from irritations to paralysis and even death. The same toxins made toads a prominent ingredient in magic potions and witches' brews. A brew made with enough toads could be deadly.

At Kemp's witchcraft trial, the toad familiar Pigin was said to have caused illness in a boy. That a toad could make a person ill is not so unbelievable from a purely medical perspective.

Ravens, large, black and intelligent birds, feature prominently in folklore. The Norse God Odin was attended by a pair of ravens named Huginn and Muninn and Norse battle flags often depicted the birds. Hebrew folklore says that the first bird Noah sent out from the Ark was a white raven. The faithless bird learned that the waters were receding but did not return to tell Noah. As punishment, the Raven was turned black and condemned to eat carrion.

Pliny The Elder tells us that the Romans considered the Raven an evil creature:

> *Ravens are the only birds that seem to have any comprehension of the meaning of their auspices; for when the guests of Medus were assassinated, they all took their departure from Peloponnesus and the region of Attica. They are of the very worst omen when they swallow their voice, as if they were being choked.*

The Raven's association with witchcraft and Halloween likely has to do with several characteristics: First, the birds have a reputation as carrion eaters. Feasting on the dead is a ghoulish activity that awakens deep fears in man. Second is the Raven's ability to mimic human speech. An animal that can "talk" surely is suspect as a source of witchcraft. Only a creature possessed of a human or demon spirit would be able to accomplish such a feat. Finally, the Raven's black feathers mark it as a creature of the night.

Black and Norwegian rats in Europe have a deservedly bad reputation and it is not surprising that they are associated with witchcraft and Halloween horrors. Since ancient times, rats in Europe have been the omens — and the carriers — of some of mankind's worst diseases. The Black Death, perhaps the worst calamity ever to strike European civilization, was carried by the fleas of rats. The method of transmission was unknown at the time, but the increase of rats in times of pestilence did not go unnoticed. The plague, they thought, was a horror visited upon them by evil, and rats were at least the harbingers.

Rats' association with the plague may account for the widely known story of the Pied Piper of Hamelin. As the tale is told, in 1284 the town of Hamelin was suffering from an infestation of rats. To rid themselves of the pests, the town fathers hired mysterious stranger, dressed in pied (multicolored clothing), who claimed to have a solution. The man in pied then played a set of magical pipes (flutes), and charmed the rats out of town to a river, where all but one drowned. The town fathers reneged on their promise to pay the Piper, however, and in revenge he led the village's children away to a cave where they were never seen again.

While any number of Pied Piper explanations have been offered (including a pedophile serial killer) the one most relevant here is that the story is a cautionary tale about the complicity of rats in the death of children from the plague.

Even without the plague connotations, however, the rat seems a likely candidate for a witch's familiar. Like the other suspects, rats are nocturnal, and their sleek black and dark brown colors carry the taint of evil. Further the rat's high intelligence, curiosity and often near-human behaviors, such as hoarding, led some to conclude that they were possessed of the souls of the deceased.

Devils

Of all things evil on Halloween, devils are by definition, the worst. In religions around the world and through the ages, devils (or THE Devil) are the embodiment of evil. Christian tradition holds that the Devil, or Satan, is a fallen angel. In the Islamic faith, it is a being called Shaitan, which leads mankind away from God. The Hebrew Ha-Satan is one whose mission is to act as an adversary, accuser or prosecutor. It is this Satan who persecutes Job on a bet from God.

The modern word "Devil" comes from the Greek word "diabolos", which means "slanderer" or "accuser."

Satan's modern Halloween appearance, with his red tights (or red skin), horns, hooves and tail is a mix of imagery from religion, folklore and literature.

Medieval and renaissance illustrations of the Devil typically show a creature with a goat's lower body and tail, the upper body of a man, and an often goat-like head with horns. Even when the devil's head is human, it generally assumes the triangular shape of a goat's skull.

These images (minus the bat wings) bear an uncanny resemblance to the Greek deity Pan and the Roman Faunus. Pan is a god of shepherds and their flocks, nature, hunting, and as shown with the Pan flutes, music. Pan also is associated with fertility and seduction. In art, Pan is portrayed as a horned half-man, half-goat. Nor is Pan the only horned god of the pagan world. Cernunnos (Latin for "Horned One") was the horned god of the Celtic world. The Romano-British had a horned god named Cocidius.

One explanation for the resemblance is that as Christianity spread throughout Europe, its adherents tried to discredit older gods by associating them with evil.

Devils often are shown carrying a three pronged tool, described either as a "trident" or a "pitchfork." They are not the same thing. A trident is a three-pronged, barbed fishing spear, while a pitchfork is a two-to-six pronged agriculture implement used to toss (pitch) hay, leaves and other loose material.

Tridents are the symbol of the Greek god Poseidon and the Roman Neptune (and incidentally, of the Hindu god Shiva). The incorporation of the well known Poseidon's Trident into devil imagery could very well have been an attempt to discredit a pagan god.

Along with a fishing net, the trident was famously used in Roman gladiatorial games by a "retiarius." The trident was used to disarm and kill the opponent, while the net was used to entangle him. Gladiatorial games were a particular horror for early Christians, who sometimes found themselves on the wrong end of the spectacle.

The pitchfork has far fewer evil connotations. While the image of revolting peasants with their torches and pitchforks is strong, there is no reason to associate a commonplace agricultural implement with evil. Where the Devil's tool is described as a pitchfork, it likely results from confusion with the trident.

In some illustrations, the Devil has a barbed tail and great bat or dragon wings. This can be traced to the Christian Bible, where in the *Book of Revelations*, Satan is described as a great red dragon:

> *3 And there appeared another wonder in heaven; and behold a great red dragon, having seven heads and ten horns, and seven crowns upon his heads.*
>
> *4 And his tail drew the third part of the stars of heaven, and did cast them to the earth: and the dragon stood before the woman which was ready to be delivered, for to devour her child as soon as it was born.*

5 And she brought forth a man child, who was to rule all nations with a rod of iron: and her child was caught up unto God, and to his throne.

6 And the woman fled into the wilderness, where she hath a place prepared of God, that they should feed her there a thousand two hundred and threescore days.

7 And there was war in heaven: Michael and his angels fought against the dragon; and the dragon fought and his angels,

8 And prevailed not; neither was their place found any more in heaven.

9 And the great dragon was cast out, that old serpent, called the Devil, and Satan, which deceiveth the whole world: he was cast out into the earth, and his angels were cast out with him.

This may also explain why the Devil often is shown in a red costume or with red skin.

Productions of the story of *Faust* also influenced modern Devil imagery. *Faust* is a German folktale about an astronomer who sells his soul to the Devil in exchange for knowledge. Naturally, this does not turn out well. The inspiration for the story has been identified variously as Dr. Johann Faust (1480 - 1540), a German alchemist; Dr. John Dee (1507 - 1608), an English court alchemist; or even Johann Fust, Johannes Gutenberg's business partner . The story was popular in Germany, finding its way into plays and puppet theater. Later, it was reworked by a great many authors including a 1604 version by playwright Christopher Marlowe (sometimes thought to be the real author of Shakespeare's plays) and one written Johann Wolfgang von Goethe around 1800. The 1955 musical *Damn Yankees* is based on the *Faust* story.

The *Faust* of Marlowe and Goethe is set in the 1600s, so the Devil was dressed in the style of a nobleman of that day: tights, doublet, cape, cavalier mustache and goatee. Early color illustrations of the costume worm by the actors in the play show that it was red. This, then, is the image most seen in today's Halloween devil costumes.

Another depiction of the Devils that has not generally survived to this day is that of a man dressed in black (although it may survive in the Men in Black meme). In these descriptions, the Devil may also have jet black skin (not African). The description is particularly prevalent in descriptions of the devil that emerged from witchcraft trials. As late as 1932, the horror writer H.P. Lovecraft described the devil as a black man (again, not African in origin).

Fortune Telling

Fortune telling at modern Halloween celebrations adds an air of magic and mystery to otherwise light-hearted occasions. Fortune tellers, sometimes dressed in gypsy costumes, gaze into crystal balls, read palms and tea leaves or lay out tarot cards. Ouija boards are used to answer questions about the future. Apple peels and nuts are used in divination games.

It is all fun and games, but the tradition — as with so many things Halloween — has centuries of often dark precedents.

For the Celts, Samhain was a powerful occasion for divining the future. In the sacred fires and the entrails of sacrifices, Druids purported to predict the return of spring, the bounty of the next summer's crops and the success of the community.

Thankfully, the practice of reading the entrails of sacrifices generally has not survived. Reading the future in flames, on the other hand, does. Gazing into a candle flame, or into a mirror lit only by a candle is said to reveal the petitioner's future. Modern fortune telling party games also sometimes involve dripping candle wax on a table. The wax is said to form letters that provide clues to the future.

Other fortune telling traditions draw on the Roman harvest festival of Pomona. These usually feature apples and nuts.

Bobbing for Apples originally was a divination game. Played by groups of young girls, the first to grab an apple with their teeth was predicted to be the first to marry.

Another apple-based tradition says that if a young woman peels an apple in one long continuous ribbon, and then throws it over her shoulder, it will upon landing form the first initial of her true love. Just as some fortune tellers read tea leaves, others would split open an apple and "read" the seed pattern within for clues about the future.

And, in a blending of Celt and Roman traditions, girls seeking their future husband were instructed to pare an apple by candlelight while sitting in front of a mirror. The girl's future husband will appear as a reflective apparition. The appearance of a skull, however, indicates that she will die before matrimony. Another fortune telling game involving apples and fire instructs young girls to suspend an apple on a string over the flames. The order in which the apples fall into the fire indicates the order of marriage.

Throwing a hazelnut into a fire was said to predict the course of future love. If the nut split loudly, the petitioner's marriage would be a happy one. A nut that simply burned indicated an unhappy arrangement. Cracking a walnut was said to offer similar results. If the nut split cleanly, the marriage would be successful. A splintered walnut indicated misfortune in love.

In spite of Puritan admonitions, fortune telling games were common in Colonial New England. In fact, one of the precipitating events of the Salem Witch Trials was a visit of young village girls to participate in fortune telling with the slave woman Tituba. Elsewhere in Colonial America, fortune telling was practiced both in earnest, and as a form of entertainment.

Through the Victorian period, much of the fortune telling seems focused on revealing the future of loves and marriages. Following the First World War, however, séances, often became attempts by families to reconnect with their fallen. Harry Houdini, the famous magician and escape artist spent a good deal of his time debunking séance con-men.

Ouija boards (the patent is owned by Hasbro) have been part of American Halloweens since the first commercial boards were sold in the 19th century. Also known as "spirit," or "talking" boards, these belong to a branch of the fortune telling family known as "automatic writing" (the automation supposedly being supplied by spirits).

Spirit boards typically have an arrangement of letters and numbers printed on their surface. To consult the spirits, participants place their fingers on a small movable pointer. A question is asked, and the pointer slides across the board, pausing at the letters to spell out an answer.

Spirit boards actually date back to 12th century China, and are mentioned in several documents of the Song dynasty. In 19th century America, a variety of boards were manufactured. Finally a patent was filed in 1890 for a board with a specific letter configuration and planchette (movable pointer). Production of the existing Ouija board began in 1901. Legend has it that Ouija is Egyptian for "good luck." It also is said to come from the French (Oui) and German (ja) words for "yes." The patents were sold to Parker Brothers in 1966, and Parker Brothers was subsequently sold to Hasbro in 1991.

Another modern "spirit writing" toy is the "Magic 8-Ball." The inventor, Albert Carter, apparently was inspired by the work of his mother, a clairvoyant. He was issued a patent in 1944, and the modern version appeared in 1950. To use the ball, the petitioner asks a yes or no question, then shakes the ball and looks to see what answer is revealed in the window. The Magic 8-Ball's key component is a 20-sided die floating in a dark liquid. The die has ten "yes" answers, five "no" and five "neutral."

Crystal Balls are globes of beryl, glass or quartz used to divine the future. The art of gazing into such a ball, sometimes called scrying, likely has been practiced as long as the technology to make such balls has existed. Queen Elizabeth's court astrologer/magician/scientist Dr. John Dee (1507 - 1628) was noted for his use of crystals, so crystal balls are at least that old. Scrying into balls echos a still earlier practice of gazing into still pools of water, which are sometimes called "scrying pools"

Tarot Cards originally were intended not as fortune telling tools, but as game components. Tarot games date from the 1400s and perhaps as far back as the 1200s. The games include the Italian Taroccini and French Tarot. Tarot cards seem to have acquired mystic status as early as the 1500s, and certainly by late 1700s. In spite of rumors, the cards almost surely have no connection to ancient Egypt or other cultures of antiquity.

A Tarot card decks differs significantly from a "standard" playing card deck. There are four suits (swords, staves, cups and coins) with fourteen cards each (one through ten, plus king, queen, knight and jack) that are known to fortune tellers as the Minor Arcana. In addition there are 22 separate cards known as the Major Arcana. These include The Magician, The High Priestess, The Empress, The Emperor, The Hierophant, The Lovers, The Chariot, Strength, The Hermit, Wheel of Fortune, Justice, The Hanged Man, Death, Temperance, The Devil, The Tower, The Star, The Moon, The Sun, Judgment, The World and The Fool.

Frankenstein's Monster

The limits of science — both actual and ethical — provide the theme for another of the elements of modern Halloween and horror imagery: that of the man-made monster.

The idea that man can be threatened, or even destroyed, by his own creations is an old one. The Jewish folktale of the Golem tells of a priest who created a servant out of clay (much as God created Adam out of clay). To activate the Golem, the priest wrote the word "Emeth" (life) on its forehead. Things work out for a while, but eventually the Golem rebels and the priest is forced to destroy it. He tricks it into bending over so that he can erase the "E", converting the word to "meth" (death). The Golem immediately melts back into a large lump of clay, killing the priest.

Mary Shelley's 1818 novel Frankenstein is the classic of the genre - and one that provides seemingly endless Halloween fun. No set of Halloween decorations is complete without at least one flat headed, green monster with bolts in its neck.

In Shelley's novel, Victor Von Frankenstein is a doctor who becomes obsessed with the secrets of life. Through the course of his experiments, Frankenstein brings to life a creature, which remains nameless throughout the novel. Details of the creation are not forthcoming, but it is not entirely a success. Hoping to create something beautiful, Frankenstein instead produces a monster.

Horrified by the results, Frankenstein rejects the monster and leaves it to its own devices. Then, Frankenstein's young brother William is murdered, and the nanny is hung for the crime. The Doctor, however, begins to suspect his creation is the perpetrator. Eventually, the monster returns to Frankenstein to tell its tale. Articulate (unlike the creatures in the movies) and highly intelligent, the creature describes its observations of the human race and its perhaps accidental murder of the boy William. Having been rejected by humanity for his appearance, the creature now wants Frankenstein to make him a mate.

Fearing for his life, Frankenstein begins a second creature. Then, realizing that he could potentially start a race of monsters, Frankenstein destroys his unfinished work. Enraged, the monster kills Frankenstein's assistant and the doctor's new wife. Knowing that he must destroy his creation, Frankenstein sets off in pursuit of the creature. The chase leads to the Arctic Circle, where, exhausted, Frankenstein dies.

As the novel closes, the ship's captain discovers the creature mourning over Frankenstein's body. The creature, distraught, heads off into the ice:

"Farewell! I leave you, and in you the last of humankind whom these eyes will ever behold. Farewell, Frankenstein! If thou wert yet alive and yet cherished a desire of revenge against me, it would be better satiated in my life than in my destruction. But it was not so; thou didst seek my extinction, that I might not cause greater wretchedness; and if yet, in some mode unknown to me, thou hadst not ceased to think and feel, thou wouldst not desire against me a vengeance greater than that which I feel. Blasted as thou wert, my agony was still superior to thine, for the bitter sting of remorse will not cease to rankle in my wounds until death shall close them forever.

"But soon," he cried with sad and solemn enthusiasm, "I shall die, and what I now feel be no longer felt. Soon these burning miseries will be extinct. I shall ascend my funeral pile triumphantly and exult in the agony of the torturing flames. The light of that conflagration will fade away; my ashes will be swept into the sea by the winds. My spirit will sleep in peace, or if it thinks, it will not surely think thus. Farewell."

He sprang from the cabin window as he said this, upon the ice raft which lay close to the vessel. He was soon borne away by the waves and lost in darkness and distance.

Since its publication - just before Shelley's 21st birthday - the story of Frankenstein has been told and retold in hundreds of plays, movies, comics and novels. Most got it all wrong and missed the main points of the novel.

A clue to Shelley's intent lies in the full title of the book: *Frankenstein, or A Modern Prometheus.* In Greek mythology, Prometheus is the Titan who stole fire for humans' use, bringing them light and warmth. His punishment for the theft is eternal torment. He was bound to a rock, where each day an Eagle would eat his liver. Each night, the liver would grow back.

The novel touches on a wide variety of themes. Shelley presents deep questions about religion, morality, science and knowledge. For example, in creating life, Frankenstein is playing God. The monster, a creature outside of God's creation, struggles with the concept of humanity, and must develop its own moral code.

Grand Master Science fiction writer Brian Aldiss contends that Frankenstein was the first modern science fiction story. Frankenstein is no victim of magical forces, but deliberately uses modern (for the time) science to achieve results that have real consequences, Aldiss says.

Note that, despite what popular culture would have us believe, the creature's name is not "Frankenstein" or (worse) "Frankie." Frankenstein is the name of the Doctor. Shelley apparently declined to give the creature a name to emphasize the idea that it has no place in God's plan. It is referred to variously as "creature", "monster", "Fiend", "wretch" and "it"

The monster, however, in several places compares himself to the biblical Adam, telling Frankenstein "I ought to be thy Adam." Several authors have taken this to indicate that the creature's name was indeed "Adam."

It is also worth noting that the creature in the novel looks nothing like the square-headed, bolt-necked being from the 1931 Universal Pictures movie. That image of the monster was created by Hollywood makeup man Frank Pierce for actor Boris Karloff, who has become the definitive Frankenstein.

Here is how Shelley describes him:

> *His yellow skin scarcely covered the work of muscles and arteries beneath; his hair was of a lustrous black, and flowing; his teeth of a pearly whiteness; but these luxuriances only formed a more horrid contrast with his watery eyes, that seemed almost of the same colour as the dun-white sockets in which they were set, his shrivelled complexion and straight black lips.*

Some more recent films have tried to more accurately recreate Shelley's original image, but they were not particularly successful. Karloff's portrayal of the monster is the definitive one for our time.

Frankenstein was written by the young Mary Wollstonecraft Godwin while she and her lover, the poet Percy Bysshe Shelley were on vacation in Geneva, Switzerland. There, Lord Byron challenged them, and another houseguest, John Polidori to see who could write the best ghost story. Byron and Percey Shelley apparently wrote forgettable pieces, but Mary Wollstonecraft Godwin's work became legendary. (Polidori's work also has had long-lasting impact.)

Mary Wollstonecraft Godwin later married Percey Shelley after the suicide of his wife. Today, the byline of the novel reads Mary Shelley.

Ghosts

There may be no more classic Halloween costume than the bed sheet ghost.

Belief in ghosts is a nearly universal concept. While the description and behavior of these spirits vary across time and geography, they are nearly always thought to be the spirits of the deceased. Some make themselves known in corporeal form, while others are said to appear as vague shapes or shadows. Mysterious noises, or the movement of objects also are said to be signs of ghosts.

In some cultures, spirits are friendly and helpful. In others, they are objects of dread. It is a culture of fear that lay behind the original Halloween rituals of Samhain. On that night, the dead were said once more to walk, to menace the Earth and perhaps occupy the bodies of the living.

In Japan, there is a ghost called a Yurei that remains behind to avenge a wrongful death. They appear floating in air, dressed in white kimonos, with black, disheveled hair. India has its bhoot, another type of avenging spirit. China has a great variety of ghosts, which makes sense, given the traditional ancestor worship.

Most people do not become ghosts, or the world would quickly be overrun with spooks. Therefore it makes sense that ghosts only appear on certain nights, or under unusual circumstances. Traditional ghost stories speak of people remaining on Earth as a ghost to seek revenge for a wrong, or as punishment for a crime they committed.

Other ghosts may cross over to the land of the living to deliver warnings or complete some unfinished business. Ghosts also are associated with particularly tragic deaths.

The word "ghost" comes from the Old English "gast", which itself is borrowed from the German "geist", or spirit. Spirit itself comes from the Latin word spiritus, meaning soul, courage, vigor or breath.

The roots of the belief that ghosts and spirits are translucent and incorporeal probably can be seen in the words' origins. Ghost means spirit and spirit means breath. In Genesis, God brings Adam to life with a breath:

> *And the LORD God formed man of the dust of the ground, and breathed into his nostrils the breath of life; and man became a living soul.*

Thus, it is the breath that brings life. The body had been constructed but was not alive until it received God's breath. Upon death, the tangible body remains, but no longer breathes or responds. No one has seen the animating force leave, so the spirit, like God, must be intangible.

There may also be a connection between the stereotypical ghostly form and the breath that sometimes can be seen as mist in cooler weather.

Medieval Europeans thought of ghosts as either souls or demons. The souls were of people stuck in Purgatory until they atoned for their sins in life. Like the Celtic spirits of Samhain, the demons' only goal was to torment the living.

During the Renaissance, William Shakespeare took full advantage of ghosts for dramatic effect. Ghosts appear in Julius Caesar, Hamlet, Richard III, Cymbeline, All's Well that Ends Well, Anthony and Cleopatra, Henry V, Romeo and Juliet and Much Ado About Nothing.

Colonial America — in spite of the influence of the Enlightenment — had a strong belief in ghosts … and witches … and vampires. Today, Colonial Williamsburg, the wonderful living history town and museum in Virginia, offers historical "ghost walks" of the many 17th and 18th century buildings. Shield's Tavern, for example, is said to be haunted by the vengeful ghost of a man murdered in the building. The Peyton Randolph House, on the other hand, is said to be visited by the tragic spirit of a young man of promise. The nearby College of William and Mary, which dates to 1693, is allegedly haunted by many spirits.

Spiritualism is the belief that ghosts are willing and able to communicate with the world of the living. This is primarily done through séances, in which "mediums" act as a conduit. The mediums may talk directly to the spirits, interpret "spirit tapping," perform "spirit writing," or allow themselves to be temporarily possessed.

While it claims much older roots, the spiritualism movement gained widespread popularity in the mid-1800s, when it was reported that the Fox sisters — Leah, Margaret and Kate — of Hydesville, New York, were able to communicate with a ghost. The spirit — that of a murdered man who had lived in their house — sent the two younger sisters messages through rapping noises. Others soon took up the banner and séances became common place. It is as this time that the first Ouija boards became commercially available. Eventually, millions were caught up in the spiritualism movement. Mary Todd Lincoln and Queen Victoria both were to have participated in séances, presumably to contact the ghosts of lost loved ones.

The movement largely collapsed in the late 1800s when the Fox sisters confessed that it was a hoax, and several other prominent spiritualists were proven to be frauds.

Spiritualism and séances once again became popular during the First World War, as people tried to cope with the unprecedented loss of life. Sir Arthur Conan Doyle, creator of Sherlock Holmes, was a prominent supporter. Doyle, devastated by the loss of family and friends, apparently found solace in the thought that he could still communicate with them. Doyle gave public lectures, and contributed articles on the subject.

Opposed to the rising spiritualist movement was Harry Houdini, one of the greatest "escape artists" of all time. Like Doyle, Houdini had first sought comfort from spiritualism in contacting his deceased mother. His training as a magician, however, quickly led him to discover the tricks the "mediums" used to simulate spirit contact. Houdini then went on a crusade to bring the spiritualist movement down. Houdini's untimely (and somewhat mysterious) death on Halloween night 1926 put an end to his pursuit.

Before his death, Houdini had made arrangements with his wife that if he were able to escape from the afterlife, or communicate from the other side, he would transmit a secret code. After ten years of futile waiting and listening, his wife gave up.

Spook, which often is used as a substitute for "ghost," is one of many Dutch words that entered the American lexicon via settlers in New York in the 1600s and 1700s. Others are "cookie", "boss" and even "Santa Claus."

The "Haunted House," inhabited by the spirits of former occupants, is a strong Halloween image. The building is not always a single-family dwelling, though. The Tower of London is said to be thoroughly haunted, as are the US White House (a residence, office building and museum) and Capitol building. Still, the most common haunted house image is that of a dilapidated Victorian era structure, with large porches, towers and turrets, surrounded by a wrought iron fence.

Among the signs of a haunted house are the appearance of spirits, mysterious noises and cold spots in rooms. Objects in haunted houses move on their own, pictures tilt constantly and walls and floors develop mysterious stains.

As anyone who has ever lived in one can attest, old houses make a lot of noises. Loose joints, and uneven settling shift with temperature changes. Poor insulation and inefficient heating create both cold and hot spots. Uneven floors and walls can make objects shift positions and pictures tilt. It has even been suggested that ghostly sightings are in fact hallucinations resulting from carbon monoxide poisoning from old furnaces and gas lamp fixtures.

Poltergeists — "noisy ghosts" in German — are spirits known for their destructive behavior. Unlike ghosts who haunt a location, these often are said to haunt a particular person. Poltergeists may throw objects, bang on furniture and walls, or even physically attack people with bites and pinches. The ghosts have captured the popular imagination first with Noel Coward's 1941 play, *Blythe Spirit*, and later with the *Poltergeist* series of movies (1982, 1986 and 1988). They also are featured in the S.T.A.L.K.E.R video game series.

Ghouls

Ghoul comes from the Arabic "ghul", which means "demon." The ghul is a creature that inhabits graveyards and other barren places. In some stories, the ghul can shift shapes, often becoming a hyena, a particularly feared animal of desert and veldt. Ghuls seem to be particularly fond of eating children, a behavior which also has been ascribed to hyenas.

In modern usage, a ghoul is a person who takes delight in things that are revolting or offensive, linked no doubt to the cannibalistic tendencies of mythical ghouls.

Ghouls make their first appearance in written literature in the *Thousand and One Arabian Nights*. In the story *The History of Gherib and His Brother Agib*, a prince does battle against the Ghoul of the Mountains and his followers. In *The Story of Sidi-Nouman*, a man is horrified to find his new wife consorting with ghouls:

> *It was bright moonlight, so I easily managed to keep her in sight, till she entered a cemetery not far from the house. There I hid myself under the shadow of the wall, and crouched down cautiously; and hardly was I concealed, when I saw my wife approaching in company with a ghoul--one of those demons which, as your Highness is aware, wander about the country*

making their lairs in deserted buildings and springing out upon unwary travelers whose flesh they eat. If no live being goes their way, they then betake themselves to the cemeteries, and feed upon the dead bodies.

I was nearly struck dumb with horror on seeing my wife with this hideous female ghoul. They passed by me without noticing me, began to dig up a corpse which had been buried that day, and then sat down on the edge of the grave, to enjoy their frightful repast, talking quietly and cheerfully all the while, though I was too far off to hear what they said. When they had finished, they threw back the body into the grave, and heaped back the earth upon it. I made no effort to disturb them, and returned quickly to the house, when I took care to leave the door open, as I had previously found it. Then I got back into bed, and pretended to sleep soundly.

As the *Arabian Nights* made their way to Europe, first in a 1704 French translation and perhaps most notably through a translation by Richard Burton (1885), the ghouls, jinn and other creatures in the stories were incorporated in western folklore.

Hans Christian Anderson, for example, borrows ghouls for his story *The Wild Swans*. In this, the heroine Eliza must gather nettles from a graveyard:

Then with a trembling heart, as if she were about to perform a wicked deed, she crept into the garden in the broad moonlight, and passed through the narrow walks and the deserted streets, till she reached the churchyard. Then she saw on one of the broad tombstones a group of ghouls. These hideous creatures took off their rags, as if they intended to bathe, and then clawing open the fresh graves with their long, skinny fingers, pulled out the dead bodies and ate the flesh! Eliza had to pass close by them, and they fixed their wicked glances upon her, but she prayed silently, gathered the burning nettles, and carried them home with her to the castle.

Edgar Allan Poe mentions ghouls in his 1848 poem, *The Bells*, and H.P. Lovecraft describes them as bestial underground dwellers who eat human flesh. In J.K Rowling's *Harry Potter* series, however, they are depicted as mostly harmless. One of the significant villains in the Batman series is Ra's al-Ghoul, translated in the comics as "The Demon's Head."

Ghouls in modern literature are generally described as emaciated, sickly grey and dressed in tatters. In Arabian literature, they had donkey hooves when not in their shape-shifting forms.

Goblins

Goblin is a catch-all term for various species of elfin creatures. Appearing in folklore around the world, they vary widely in appearance and have personalities that range from helpful to downright evil.

The word "goblin" has uncertain origins. One thought is that comes from the old French "gobelin." Another relates it to the German "kobold." Kobold in turn comes from Greek word "kobalos", meaning rogue. Finally, the word may be a corruption of "Nibelung," or "Nybling," a Germanic-Norse race of dwarves.

The typical goblin of Halloween imagery — a small green elf-like creature — does not seem to have a parallel in folklore. Goblins are are instead more typically small hairy creatures with misshapen human features. Among the species encountered in folklore are boggards, brownies, bugbears, hobgoblins, spriggans and trows.

A boggart is described as a small, hairy and smelly creature that inhabits human homes. They are blamed for all number of common household misfortunes such as spoiled milk, broken dishes and objects that cannot be found at the moment they are needed. They are also known as boggles. Boggarts sometimes could be appeased with gifts of food and drink.

Brownies are helpful household goblins. Hard working and dedicated to their families, they are rarely if ever seen. Brownies work at night and are rewarded with gifts of food. Many households left a ceremonial "seat" next to the fireplace for the household brownie. Some stories say brownies will disappear if they believe the gifts actually are "payments." The helpful nature of the Brownie is behind the name of the Girl Scout group.

A bugbear is a frightening sort of goblin that eats naughty children. It is said to inhabit the woods and resemble a bear (again, reinforcing the traditional notion of goblins as hairy creatures). "Bugaboo" and "Bogey-Man" likely are derivatives of "Bugbear." The word "Bugbear" itself from either the English "bugge" (frightening thing), the Welsh "bwg" (goblin) or the Scottish "bogill" (goblin).

Hobgoblins are similar to Brownies, but with a mischievous nature. While they might do some work about the house, they also could be responsible for playing tricks, such as spoiling milk. Like other goblins of lore, they are described as small, hairy folk. The story of the *Shoemaker and the Elves* likely describes hobgoblins. Tradition says that if a hobgoblin is giving clothing, they will vanish.

Shakespeare's Puck from *A Midsummer Nights' Dream* is a sort of hobgoblin. In English folklore, Puck also is known as Robin Goodfellow and was identified as a hobgoblin by one of the play's fairies:

Either I mistake your shape and making quite,

Or else you are that shrewd and knavish sprite

Call'd Robin Goodfellow: are not you he

That frights the maidens of the villagery;

Skim milk, and sometimes labour in the quern

And bootless make the breathless housewife churn;

And sometime make the drink to bear no barm;

Mislead night-wanderers, laughing at their harm?

Those that Hobgoblin call you and sweet Puck,

You do their work, and they shall have good luck:

Are not you he?

Spriggans are goblins of the forest. They were said to be small, quite ugly and tough and were used to guard fairy treasures. They also were blamed for stealing human children and leaving changelings in their place.

Trows, originating in Orkney and the Shetland Islands, are said to be ugly, stunted and hairy. Living in caves and barrows during the day, they will visit houses by night. Some stories say that they can only walk backwards.

If there is a precedent for the green skinned goblin, it might be in the Green Men. These were forest deities that took the form of plants or trees. Their faces, as represented in architectural carvings seem to be composed of leaves.

One explanation for goblin stories – especially in Great Britain – is that they represent remnant populations displaced by new waves of invaders. Prehistoric Beaker people were supplanted by the Celts, who were in turn conquered by the Romans. Later, the Romano British were themselves overrun by the Angles, Saxons and Jutes, who ultimately fell to the Normans. As the Norse invaded the northern portions of the island, the Picts were driven out.

For refugee populations, woods, caves and mountains offer shelter. Night would have offered the opportunity for refugees to raid villages for needed supplies and perhaps commit some mischief for the invaders. Leaving gifts of food and drink may have served to appease the refugees in the woods, who found it easier to accept gifts than steal. That goblins are described as small (perhaps malnourished) and hairy also fits the refugee theory. These refugees would have been undernourished and unkempt.

Headless Horsemen

Headless Horsemen have figured in the imaginations of many cultures, and have now become a fixture in modern horror and Halloween celebrations. Some compilations of Grimm's Fairy Tales include an encounter with a headless horseman. Bavarian folklore apparently contain tales of Headless Horsemen who patrol the forests.

In India, a character called the Dund rides about headless, although his noggin is tied to his saddle. The Dullahan of Irish folklore is a headless spirit seen riding a headless horse. In some variants, it is a headless coachman. The Green Knight of medieval legend is beheaded by Gawain, but rides away carrying his own head.

In a 1777 work by the German poet G.A. Burger, *Der Wilde Jager*, a ghostly huntsman is condemned for his cruel demeanor on earth. He rides with his hell hounds through the woods and chases innocents. The poem is based on German folklore and in some versions, he is headless.

The best known of the Headless Horsemen, of course, appears in Washington Irving's 1820 story, *The Legend of Sleepy Hollow*. It is this version of the story that has become Halloween legend.

Irving was not above borrowing folklore for his tales, especially from the Dutch — as in his popularization of the Dutch Santa Claus. New York, originally New Amsterdam was Dutch in origins, and Irving's Knickerbocker Tales focused on their descendants.

In Irving's story, the Headless Horseman is the ghost of a Hessian who was decapitated by a cannon ball during the American Revolution. His spirit haunts the town of Sleepy Hollow.

The Hessians were mercenary soldiers from the German state of Hesse-Kassel hired by King George III to fight against the Continental Army during the American War of Independence. It was the Hessians who were caught by surprise at the Battle of Trenton after Washington crossed the Delaware River. The Hessians also featured prominently in the Saratoga Campaign in New York in 1777. The Hessian force there contained a large number of cavalry. However, in the dense upstate New York woods, the horses were abandoned, and the Hessians fought on foot. The Hessian forces under British General Johnny Burgoyne were defeated by the Colonials under Horatio Gates and Benedict Arnold.

In either case, the Hessians developed a reputation among the colonists for brutality against the local populations. Whether that was true, or only propaganda, is unclear. Their reputation, however, plays a part in the Legend of Sleepy Hollow.

The Washington Irving tale of horror is well known. It is set in the town of Sleepy Hollow, which, Irving reveals early in the story, is a magical place haunted by the spirit of a headless Hessian trooper. The plot revolves around a schoolmaster named Ichabod Crane, who is in pursuit of Katrina van Tassel, a wealth heiress. Unfortunately for the skinny and somewhat meek Crane, his competition for Katrina is the local bully, Brom Bones.

The subject of the horseman comes up at a local party, where the various young men of Sleepy Hollow are telling ghost stories. Brom Bones claims to have raced the Headless Horseman for the stakes of a bowl of punch. In the race, he claims that the Horseman was unable to cross the water under the town's bridge. Even with this lightheartedness, however, Crane is nervous.

Irving notes that the time of year is autumn, but does not specify whether or not it is Halloween.

On the way home from the party, Crane imagines all sorts of scary things in the woods. Eventually, he is joined by another rider. When Crane recognizes the Horseman, he flees, hoping to reach the bridge for the safety of town.

Crane nearly makes it. But, at the last minute, the Horseman throws his head, knocking the schoolteacher from his mount. That is the last we hear of Crane. The next morning his horse is found, as is a shattered pumpkin, but there is no sign of the schoolteacher. His fate is never actually revealed by the storyteller.

Modern audiences have been heavily influenced by the Disney short (1958) and by the Tim Burton movie (1999), which differs significantly from the Irving version.

The Jack O'Lantern

The Jack O' Lantern has its origins in Irish folklore:

According to the story, there once was a ne'er-do-well named Jack. An infamous drunk, he could generally be found at the local pub. One day, Jack is sitting in the bar when along comes the Devil.

"Jack," he says. "It is time to go."

Jack begins to whine. "Oh Devil," he says. "I'd love to go with you, but first, I'd like to have just one more drink."

"Fine," says the Devil. "Go ahead."

Jack fishes in his pocket and pulls out his change purse. It is empty. "Oh Devil," Jack says. "I once heard that you could change yourself into anything you like."

"It is true," says the Devil.

"Well," says Jack. "Could you turn yourself into a coin so I could buy another drink. Then you could change yourself back and cheat the barkeep out of his money."

The idea of cheating the barkeep appealed to the Devil, so he changed into a coin. And quick as a wink, Jack picked up the coin and put it into his purse. Then he took out his knife and carved a cross on it.

The Devil was stuck inside.

"Let me out!" he said.

"Not until we make a deal," said Jack. "I have some unfinished business. If I let you out, you must promise to give me another year."

The Devil grumbled, but agreed to the terms. And Jack opened the purse and dumped him out. The Devil then went away.

A year later, Jack was sitting in the same pub, when along came the Devil.

"Your year is up," The Devil said. "No more tricks now, lets go."

Jack followed the Devil out of the Pub and was on his way to Hell. But along the way, he passed an apple tree

"Oh Devil," said Jack. "Before I go to Hell, I would really love to have an apple to eat."

The Devil did not see any harm in this, so he agreed. Jack tried to reach an apple, but it was to high for him to reach. He tried to climb the tree, but slid back down.

Disgusted and impatient, the Devil jumped into the tree to get the apple for Jack. And quick as a wink, Jack whipped out his pocket knife and carved a cross on the tree trunk.
The Devil was stuck in the tree.

"Let me down!" he said.

"Not until we make a deal," Jack said. "You must promise to go away and never bother me again."

"Be careful what you wish for," the Devil said.

"Just promise to leave me alone," Jack repeated.

The Devil agreed, and Jack carved out the Cross. The Devil jumped down and went away.

And after that, Jack lived a very, very, very, very, very, very, very long life. So long in fact, that he began to tire of living. So Jack went in search of Heaven. But when he found the Pearly Gates, St. Peter refuses to let him in.

So Jack went in search of Hell. When he got to the fiery gates, the Devil was waiting.

"Oh, Devil," Jack said. "I'm so tired of living. I'm old and I'm cold and I want to end it all."

The Devil just laughed. "Don't you remember our deal? I promised to leave you alone forever."

"But where will I go?" Jack asked. "I'm lost, it is dark, and I don't know the way."

"Here," said the Devil, "take this!" And he reached down and grabbed a big scoop of Hell. And he threw it to Jack.

Jack caught it, but it was so hot that he tried to drop it. Only he couldn't. No matter how much he tried, the stuff stuck to his fingers. So he ran out into the dark fields outside of Hell and grabbed a turnip. He took out his pocketknife, and quick as a flash, carved out the inside, and dropped the hellfire inside. Then, he carved a couple of holes in the front of the turnip and wandered off, using it as a lantern.

So Jack of the Lantern - Jack O'Lantern — wanders to this very day, carrying his hellish light with him.

The Irish used turnips for their Jack O'Lanterns in Ireland. But when they reached America, they found that pumpkins were more plentiful, and made a better lantern. And so the Jack O'Lantern pumpkin was born.

Mad Scientists

The theme of science gone amok is pervasive in 19th and 20th Century Halloween iconography and at the heart of many of these stories is the "mad scientist." Conducting experiments in things man was not meant to know, the Mad Scientist may be evil or well intentioned, but his results are generally not for the best.

The most famous name in mad scientists probably is Frankenstein, from the Mary Shelley story of the same name. Frankenstein plays God and creates life, only to have it turn on him and destroy his life. (You can read more in the Frankenstein chapter in this book).

While the Dr. Frankenstein of the book is a somewhat sympathetic character and his methods are not described, the Hollywood version is the one that most people recognize. Wild haired and eyed, in a lab coat with bubbling chemicals and strange electrical devices in the background, Hollywood's Dr. Frankenstein is the one that has found its way into our Halloweens.

Another famous example of the mad scientist story is Robert Louis Stevenson's 1886 novel *The Strange Case of Dr. Jekyll and Mr. Hyde*. In this, Dr. Jekyll creates a formula that separates man's good aspect from his bad. Testing the potion on himself, he eventually finds himself turning uncontrollably (or perhaps even willingly) into the evil Mr. Hyde.

The story begins with a series of brutal assaults by a man named Hyde, who inexplicably has a connection to the respectable Doctor Jekyll. Hyde runs over a young girl and then pays the family off with a check drawn on Jekyll's account. Later, Hyde beats to death a member of Parliament and clues again point to Jekyll's involvement.

Hyde continues his nightly appearances, even as Jekyll withdraws from his friends, finally locking himself in his laboratory. Worried, his friends break into the lab, to find Hyde, having apparently committed suicide in Jekyll's clothes.

A letter from Jekyll, found on the scene, reveals the surprise ending. Jekyll, a man tempted by dark thoughts, had initially enjoyed his freedom from moral restrictions. However, Jekyll found himself turning into Hyde even without the formula. Jekyll writes in his letter that he knows he will soon become Hyde permanently and wonders if Hyde will face the law, or choose suicide.

The Strange Case of Dr. Jekyll and Mr. Hyde has inspired a great deal of analysis and literary criticism. Stevenson apparently conceived of it as an allegorical novel, but others have pegged *Jekyll* as a detective story, or as a tale of gothic horror. One big question surrounds the nature of Mr. Hyde. Does Jekyll actually transform into a different person, or is Mr. Hyde just Jekyll's true dark nature? Is the story about schizophrenia or some sort of Freudian conflict between conscious and unconscious? Or is the story one of larger issues about divisions in social class in Victorian England and Scotland. Opinions vary.

In any case, it is clear that at the heart of the tale lies a man of science who, in attempting to banish evil, instead brings it forth. That is the classic mad scientist.

The *Strange Case of Dr. Jekyll and Mr. Hyde* was an immediate success, and stage adaptations began within the year. There have been more than one hundred film versions, and even more on radio and television.

It is safe to say, however, that the vast majority of these have missed a central element of the novel: the mystery. In the adaptations, it is clear from the outset that Jekyll is turning into Hyde. In the novel, the identity of Hyde is a mystery that is revealed only in the shocking ending.

In addition to the direct adaptations, the Jekyll and Hyde story is at the core of other literary and pop culture creations, such as the comic book characters "Hulk" and the Batman villain "Two-Face." Indeed, the dual identities of many costumed heroes — mild mannered folk with violent alter-egos — echo that of Jekyll and Hyde.

The impact of the novel on our imaginations has been profound. Comedic adaptations abound, as do references to the story in every medium imaginable. Children's cartoons are rife with images of a scientist who drinks a potion and turns into a monster. Indeed, the very phrase, " Jekyll and Hyde" has become a common saying.

H.G. Wells, author of *War of the Worlds* and *Time Machine*, published the lesser known *Island of Dr. Moreau* in 1896. In this novel, the Doctor is a vivisectionist who, on an isolated island, conducts experiments to combine humans and animals.

Dr. Moreau is told from the perspective of Edward Prendick, who as the result of a shipwreck finds himself stranded on the island. Prendick is given refuge by Dr. Moreau, who had come to the island after fleeing vivisection charges in England. In the surrounding Jungle, Prendick encounters some of Moreau's creations: the Beast Folk, animals that have been transformed to near human form. Eventually, Moreau is killed by one of his creations. Prendick, now alone, lives with the Beast Folk, but as time passes finds them regressing back into animals. Frightened, he takes advantage of a boat that has drifted to the island and uses it to escape.

Like *Jekyll*, *Moreau* had been adapted to the screen (though not nearly as frequently). Most famous of these are the 1932 *Island of Lost Souls* with Charles Laughton and Bela Lugosi and a 1996 version with Marlon Brando and Val Kilmer. Variations on the theme include the popular *Planet of the Apes* series, with its anthropomorphized apes. As with Moreau, after being raised up, the creations turn on their creators.

Wells' *Invisible Man* also features a scientist whose experiments go very wrong.

Much of the mad scientist imagery can be traced to Fritz Lang's 1927 silent, black and white movie classic, *Metropolis*. Rotwang, the film's mad scientist, with his wild hair and eyes and distinctive clothing, presides over a laboratory of weird electrical gear, bubbling chemicals, levers, buttons and controls.

The rise of the mad scientist as a villain probably begins with the First World War, when science's potential for mass destruction became painfully evident. Machine guns, aircraft and poison gas transformed war from the "Sport of Kings" to scientific slaughter. The Second World War continued that trend, and came complete with a cast of real-life evil mad scientists, as Nazi and Japanese scientists practiced unspeakable horrors on their victims.

The Nazi connection from the Second World War probably explains the often fascist leanings (and attire) of fictional modern mad scientists.

As the Cold War developed, the threat of the scientific destruction of all of humanity was a real possibility and the mad scientist became a staple of movies and literature. Dr. Strangelove, in the Stanley Kubrick film of the same name, surely is the apogee of the genre. Bond villains of the novels and movies also fit the mold.

Mad Scientists became staples of horror movies from the 1950s on. In *The Fly* (1958 and 1986) a scientist's experiments in teleportation go wrong, transforming him into a fly. In *Forbidden Planet*, (1956) Professor Morbeus' quest for knowledge leads to his death and the near destruction of the expedition. More recently, Dr. Tyrell in *Blade Runner* creates creatures that return to destroy him.

If there was a real-life model for a mad scientist who uses his powers for good, it might be Nikola Tesla (1856 - 1943). Tesla, a Serbian-American, invented the Tesla Coil, contributed to the modern alternating current system, developed AC brushless motors and spark plugs, produced the principles of radio communication and experimented with x rays. Tesla also claimed to have developed a "death ray." He was, also an eccentric, who believed he had received extraterrestrial communications and probably suffered from obsessive-compulsive disorder.

Mad Slashers and Psychos

A relative newcomer to the Halloween scene is the psycho / serial killer. Popularized by film series such as *Halloween* and *Friday the 13th*, they reflect any number of modern fears - just as ghost stories reflected the fears of times past. In a way, they ARE our ghost stories.

Consider the ghostlike qualities of Michael Myers in John Carpenter's classic movie *Halloween*. He slips, unseen, from location to location. He is always ready to manifest himself at the worst possible time. And, as it turns out in the innumerable sequels, he is just this side of immortal.

Freddy Krueger in *A Nightmare on Elm Street* takes it even closer to the ghost story. Freddy is the spirit of a dead child killer who manifests himself in teen aged dreams.

The frightening qualities of these Halloween horror movie serial killers is made real by the knowledge that there does not seem to be any end to man's inhumanity to man. The media serve to amplify those fears with constant coverage of sensational crime.

The original media superstar killer was Jack The Ripper. In London in 1888, the "Ripper" murdered at least six women in grisly fashion (some claim that he murdered as many as 15, but the other victims are not "official"). Some of the women were prostitutes - all were less than respectable denizens of the seedy Whitechapel neighborhood. Then, as soon as the murders started, they ended, leaving the police empty handed. The murders remain unsolved to this day.

The Ripper's name comes from a letter that he sent to the police, taunting them and containing the signature "Jack The Ripper."

In their time, the Ripper murders created a media storm, with newspapers covering every aspect of the gruesome killings. The social status of the victims just made the whole thing more salacious.

It is probably not a coincidence that, in the Halloween horror slasher movies, the bad girls die early, and the good one generally is left standing - if somewhat bloodied - at the end.

Another famous slasher killer from history is Lizzie Borden. After her parents were hacked to death with an axe in 1892, Lizzie, a 32-year-old spinster was charged with the murder. The trial became a media circus; Lizzie was eventually exonerated, but not before she became enshrined in history with the rhyme:

Lizzie Borden took an axe

And gave her mother forty whacks

When she saw what she had done

She gave her father forty one.

Of all the historical serial killers, perhaps none has had as much of an influence on fiction as Ed Gein. In the 1950s, Gein, who lived in Plainfield, Wisconsin, committed a series of gruesome and bizarre murders at his rural farmhouse.

The son of an alcoholic father and a domineering mother, Gein lived in relative isolation on a farm a few miles outside Plainfield. His mother, Augusta, was deeply (perhaps fanatically) religious, preaching to the boys about the evils of the outside world, particularly women. Gein's family died in rapid succession in the 1940s: his father in 1940, his brother Henry in a 1944 fire and his mother in 1945.

Ed, now alone, sealed off most of the house and continued his isolation. At first, his dark fantasies were satisfied by reading material of a violent and sexual nature. At some point, however, Gein began visiting cemeteries to unearth female corpses, including, according to some stories, his own mother. From some of the bodies, he claimed trophies. Others he took home, where he tanned their skin to make masks and body suits. Gein told police he made as many as forty of these trips.

Gein's grave robbing eventually turned to murder. It is unknown how many women he killed, but he was ultimately convicted of the murder of Bernice Worden in 1957. It was a tip from Worden's son that led police to the Gein farmhouse. Inside, they found Worden's disemboweled body hanging from the ceiling.

Exploration of the farm revealed a shocking hoard of body parts, some used as household items, others as jewelry, and others simply stored. As many as fifteen different women were among the pieces.

Brought to trial for Worden's murder, Gein pleaded not guilty by reason of insanity. He was kept in a series of mental hospitals until died at the age of 78 in 1984.

Gein's crimes eventually became - at least in part - the basis for a wide variety of horror literature and movies. The seemingly mild mannered Norman Bates of *Psycho (1960)* has a psychopathic mother fixation. *Texas Chainsaw Massacres* (1974) plays off the Gein legend with its house filled with body parts and the insane Leatherface with a mask of human skin. Like Gein, Buffalo Bill in *Silence of the Lambs* (1991) made masks and costumes from his victims' skin. The 1967 film, *It* features a character who converses with the rotten corpse of his mother. Several "biographical" films also have been produced.

It may not be an exaggeration to say that most modern serial killer stories can be traced to the Gein horror.

Stories of serial killers sometimes border on the ridiculous. Children in suburban Washington, D.C. in the 1970s, were terrified by rumors of a bizarre serial killer known by the not-so-frightening name of "The Bunnyman."

Rumors said that the Bunnyman inhabited the woods and swamps of suburban D.C., a large fat man wielding an axe, and wearing an Easter Bunny costume. He was a homicidal Peter Cottontail who preyed on kids and especially on teen couples parking their cars in isolated places.

The Bunnyman seems to have had his origins in the nearby town of Clifton, Virginia. Fairfax County Library Historian Brian A Conley reportedly has identified two incidents of a threatening man in a bunny costume occurred in the last weeks of October 1970. According to Conley and Washington Post reports, on October 20, 1970, USAF Academy Cadet Bennett and his fiancée were sitting in their car on Guinea Road in Burke, Virginia when a white-clad figure smashed the front passenger window. The white figure shouted "You're on private property and I have your tag number," before Bennett turned the car around and headed down the road. Later, the couple discovered a hatchet on the floor of the car. A second incident occurred on October 29 of that same year. This time, a man in a white bunny suit was spotted by a security guard on the porch of an unfinished home. The Bunnyman was chopping on the home with an axe and ran into the woods when confronted.

Four articles on the incidents eventually were printed in the Washington Post.

Given the times and the location, it is not unreasonable to assume that the "Bunny Suit" was in fact a Ku Klux Klan costume. But it has been reported that Fairfax police reports specify that the man was wearing a bunny suit. On the other hand, it is also not unreasonable that the Fairfax police would want to discount and deflect attention from a Klan presence.

Whatever the details, the story spread quickly. Local legend held that the Bunnyman not only attacked youngsters with a hatchet, but also left behind the bloody, skinned corpses of rabbits. And in an echo of the more widespread "hook" ghost story, couples reported finding hatchet scrapes on the sides of their cars after they had been parking in remote areas (and much of what is now suburban Maryland and Virginia was "remote" in those days).

The Bunnyman's apparent aversion to outsiders trespassing on his land suggests that it was a local, perhaps upset by the encroachment of real estate developments on what was until then a relatively rural and isolated area.

A well-known variant of the story pegs the initial incidents as occurring much earlier—perhaps at the turn of the century. In that version, an inmate escaped from a local Virginia insane asylum, murdered several children and left their bodies hanging from a bridge. The murderer became known as the Bunny Man when the corpses of skinned and half-eaten rabbits began turned up in the area. The bridge, a single lane auto road passing under a railroad track, is located in Clifton, Virginia. Officially called the Fairfax Station Bridge, it is now known as the Bunnyman Bridge.

Several published versions of this variant have appeared, but all have been discredited. There has never been a mental asylum in the Clifton area; investigations of newspaper and police reports have failed to turn up any documentary evidence for escaped, killer lunatic inmates.

Over the years, the story grew, and more murders were attributed to the Bunnyman, most ending with corpses hanging either from the bridge, or nearby. In Southern Maryland suburbs, bodies supposedly were found among the ruins of old Fort Washington, a large fort dating to the early 1800s.

More fantastical stories claimed that the Bunnyman is actually a giant rabbit who killed family pets. These tales echo those told about the "Goat Man," a satyr-like creature — half-man and half-goat — said to haunt Governor's Bridge Road, Lottsford Road and Fletchertown Road in Prince Georges County, Maryland. Interestingly, unlike the Bunnyman's haunts, those locations are near a state medical facility — the Glen Dale State Asylum, a tuberculosis facility whose name may have convinced some tale spinners that it was a mental institution.

Fear of the unknown. Fear of not being safe anywhere. Fear of those without "our" morals - or without any morals at all. All of these are why serial killers are such effective Halloween horror icons. While we know that ghost and vampires are figments of our imagination, we know that serial killers are all too real.

The Men In Black

The Men In Black, popularized by the movie series of the same name, are another part of Halloween alien folklore. First appearing in the 1950s, these are reportedly government agents who appear in conjunction with paranormal activities, such as UFO sightings. The agents, dressed in black, reportedly have access to much secret information and equipment. A few witnesses say that the agents often appear to have been tracking them for some time. Others describe the MIB as "out of time", wearing outdated clothing, driving classic cars and sometimes confused as to the purpose of common objects.

All of this has led some to conclude that the MIB are in fact aliens themselves.

The MIB, though, may have older folklore origins. Accounts of encounters with the Devil sometimes describe him as "The Black Man" A typical description would be of a black man with cloven hooves, sometimes naked, or as a well dressed and seemingly sophisticated individual.

The same is true in witchcraft trials. In the 1682 Bideford witch trial, Anne Wakely said that she had seen Temperance Lloyd visited by a "Black Man."

Washington Irving's 1824 story "The Devil and Tom Walker." In this scene, Tom Walker encounters the Black Man in a story set in 1727:

Tom lifted up his eyes and beheld a great black man, seated directly opposite him on the stump of a tree. He was exceedingly surprised, having neither seen nor heard any one approach, and he was still more perplexed on observing, as well as the gathering gloom would permit, that the stranger was neither negro nor Indian. It is true, he was dressed in a rude, half Indian garb, and had a red belt or sash swathed round his body, but his face was neither black nor copper colour, but swarthy and dingy and begrimed with soot, as if he had been accustomed to toil among fires and forges. He had a shock of coarse black hair, that stood out from his head in all directions; and bore an axe on his shoulder.

He scowled for a moment at Tom with a pair of great red eyes.

Nathaniel Hawthorne's *The Scarlet Letter* has a Black Man, who resides in the woods with his book of signatures. And H.P. Lovecraft, famed for his Cthulhu mythos horror stories wrote of a "Black Man" in *The Dreams of the Witch House (1933)*. The Black Man was a representative of the Devil.

The various modern explanations for the MIB seem to center around government agents sent to recover various crashed experimental aircraft, or to do damage control for other government experiments gone wrong. Another says that the entire thing originally was a hoax dreamed up by the publisher of a UFO magazine.

The Mummy

Reanimated mummies are, like the alien menace, a more recent Halloween invention. They have now become a staple in modern horror writing and movies.

Mummification has been practiced by a wide variety of cultures throughout history. Mummies are found in China, Japan, Tibet and Peru. Natural (and presumably accidental) mummies have been found in a variety of arid or frigid climates.

The most famous society that engaged in mummification was that of the ancient Egyptians. The Egyptians believed that the body was the receptacle for the Ka, which was necessary for the afterlife. Skilled embalmers prepared the body by removing the internal organs, eliminating excess moisture with salts, and then wrapping the body with linens soaked in resin.

Mummies aside, ancient Egypt long has fascinated western man. The Romans — especially in the time of Caesar — adopted Egyptian themes in their art and architecture. The ancient order of Freemasonry adopted Egyptian motifs in their organization. The involvement of some of the Founding Fathers in Freemasonry led to the inclusion of a pyramid in the Great Seal of the United States.

During his expedition to Egypt, Napoleon Bonaparte took with him teams of scientists to study the ancient civilization; Napoleon founded the Institut de l'Égypte in Cairo in 1798. It was this Institute that discovered the Rosetta Stone that finally allowed Egyptian writing to be read when it was deciphered in 1822 by Jean-Francois Champollion.

Once the mystery of Egyptian writing was unlocked, Egyptology became a Victorian era fad. It became fashionable to visit Egypt (future U.S. President Theodore Roosevelt toured Egypt as a child), where tourists picked up innumerable artifacts with which to decorate their homes. In England, public mummy unwappings was a form of entertainment. Some Victorian era religious cults, such as the Order of the Golden Dawn adopted Egyptian motifs in their ceremonies. In 1871, the composer Verdi unveiled the Egyptian themed opera, Aida.

Perhaps the first use of a mummy in science fiction or horror literature came with the 1827 publication of *The Mummy! Or A Tale Of The Twenty Second Century*, by Jane Loudon. It was a work of speculative fiction, complete with advanced technology and the scientific attempt to reanimate a long-dead mummy.

In 1869, Louisa May Alcott of Little Women fame, published a book called *Lost in A Pyramid: The Mummy's Curse*. In this books the trouble begins when an Egyptologist lights a burial chamber by burning the resin-laden body of a mummy. But there is no lumbering, murderous mummy to be found. In Alcott's book, the curse comes from some seeds taken from the tomb.

Interestingly, in one of his travelogues, Mark Twain reported that he observed mummies being used as fuel for steam engines in Egypt. But given Twain's penchant for exaggeration, it is probably best not to believe this one.

In 1890, Sir Arthur Conan Doyle (creator of Sherlock Holmes) published *The Ring of Thoth*. In that story, Egyptologist John Smith travels to the Louvre where he meets an Egyptian who has been waiting a thousand years to join his true love — now a mummy — in death.

Bram Stoker, author of Dracula, published a mummy novel in 1903. *The Jewel of the Seven Stars* is the story of an archaeologist who attempt to revive a long dead Egyptian princess.

Following the sinking of the Titanic, rumors circulated that the giant ocean liner was transporting the mummy of a priestess of Amon-Ra. A mummy's curse presumably was responsible for the liner's sinking.

Still, the idea of a Mummy's curse probably did not catch on until Howard Carter opened and excavated King Tut's tomb in 1923. The unexpected death of Lord Carnavon, Carter's sponsor, two weeks later, immediately gave rise to the idea of a curse.

Sir Arthur Conan Doyle, noted creator of Sherlock Holmes, and a great believer in mysticism did no one any favors when he speculated that "elementals" may have been involved in the Carnavon death. A publicity seeking author, Marie Cordelli, may also have added to the furor by claiming she had translations of a curse that promised dire consequences to people who opened tombs.

Carnavon's death was not so mysterious - even if it was a bit odd. By most accounts, he had been bitten by a mosquito, and then cut the bite while shaving. The wound became infected, and he died of blood poisoning.

It is weird, but hardly the stuff of a curse. One study showed that of 58 people directly involved in the opening of the tomb, only eight had died within a dozen years of the event. From an actuarial point of view, that is nothing unusual.

Moreover, it seems that an eternal curse for opening a tomb was not part of ancient Egyptian burial practices. Those that do exist seem to be aimed at the priests responsible for maintaining the tombs.

Hollywood, of course, never let the facts get in the way of a good story. In 1932, Universal Pictures released *The Mummy* starring Boris Karloff. The story involves an ancient Egyptian priest, Im-Ho-Tep, who spends his time over the centuries guarding the mummy of his lost love, Princess Anck-es-en-Amon. When the body of the Princess is taken to England, Im-Ho-Tep (now known as Ardrath Bey), follows and sets about the job of resurrecting her. This, of course, requires the body of living woman.

Rather than an outright and mysterious curse, Hollywood's curse of the mummy involves a staggering, unstoppable monster in hot pursuit of a victim. Like his portrayal of Frankenstein's monster, Boris Karloff's interpretation of the creature has left an indelible mark on our consciousness.

Today, when a mummy is portrayed in Halloween art and costumes, it is a tall, lumbering figure, arms outstretched, bandages hanging and fluttering in the air. Pure Karloff. (Real mummies have their arms bandaged to their bodies, and their feet wrapped together. They would have hopped, not walked.)

A 1959 Hammer horror film, *The Mummy*, featured Christopher Lee as the Mummy. In this version, archaeologists open the tomb of Princess Ananka and unwittingly revive her equally mummified High Priest.

In 1989, horror-romance novelist Anne Rice published *The Mummy, or Ramses The Damned.* In 1999, *The Mummy* returned for a series of films with a similar plot to their predecessors. These films, starring Brendan Fraser, are more action-adventure than horror, however.

At the core of the modern mummy stories is eternal romance. The thousand year old love of the Mummy for his princess has horrific consequences, but is undeniably tragically romantic. Perhaps that is why the character, once introduced, has become a horror and Halloween staple.

Robots

Robots are yet another theme from the realms of science fiction that have found their way into the Halloween lexicon. No modern Halloween night is complete until at least one robot, constructed of cardboard boxes and tinfoil has found its way to the door.

"Robot" comes from the Czech word Robota, meaning worker. It was first used to refer to artificial men in Karel Capek's 1920 play, Rossum's Universal Robots (RUR). In the play, robots destroy humanity after being given souls, which allow them to behave more like humans (now there is a chilling commentary).

But Capek's robots were not the first mechanical men in literature. Greek mythology tells of a bronze automaton named Talos. In 1590, the poet Edmund Spenser writes of Talus, an "iron man" who helps dispense justice in *The Faerie Queene*. Edward Ellis in 1869 wrote *The Steam Man of the Prairies*, producing what may be the first science fiction dime novel. A decade later, Harry Enton offered *Frank Reade and His Steam Man Of The Plains (1869)*, the first of a series which featured airships, submarines, electric cars and other science fiction tropes.

The beloved Oz stories from the early 1900s by L. Frank Baum feature any number of mechanical men, including the Tin Woodman, Tik-Tok and a mechanical giant who guards the entrance to the kingdom of the Nomes. These characters reflect the period's fascination with the possibilities of engineering and mechanics.

Later, there are the robots in Fritz Lang's 1927 cinematic masterpiece, Metropolis. By the 1930s, robots are a regular feature of science fiction stories in pulp magazines and cheap paperbacks. One of the most enduring of those stories is *Helen O'Loy* by Lester del Rey. Regularly cited as one of the best science fiction stories ever, it tells of the enduring romance between a robot and human.

Science Fiction writer Isaac Asimov coined the term "robotics" in his 1941 short story, "*Liar!*" That also was the story in which he created the now-well-known "Three Laws of Robotics", which state:

> *1.A robot may not harm a human being, or, through inaction, allow a human being to come to harm.*

> *2.A robot must obey the orders given to it by human beings, except where such orders would conflict with the First Law.*

> *3.A robot must protect its own existence, as long as such protection does not conflict with the First or Second Law.*

Of course, not all robots follow these laws; some have never even heard of them. Without feelings, renegade robots proceed according to a logic all of their own — and that is what makes them so scary. Robots are cold and unfeeling. People cannot appeal to their emotions. They do not care if the victims beg. Worse, their hydraulic systems make them inhumanly strong and fast.

Beginning in the 1950s, robots moved into the mainstream. Robbie-The-Robot began in the classic science fiction movie *Forbidden Planet*, but later made plenty of television appearances, including on *Lost in Space* and *The Addams Family*. He also was a much-sought-after toy.

Star Wars, of course, features perhaps the most well-known robots, the 'droids R2-D2 and C3PO. Other friendly modern 'bots include Marvin from *Hitchhiker's Guide To The Galaxy*, *Star Trek's* Data and Wall-E from the movie of the same name.

None of these, however are particularly threatening and many border on the cute. As Halloween horrors, they are failures.

Singing cowboy star Gene Autry fought an army of mechanical men in the movie serial *The Phantom Empire*. In that 1935 series, the cowboy star discovers an ancient civilization living beneath his ranch, complete with death rays and hostile robots. It was Autry's first starring role.

In *The Day The Earth Stood Still (1951)*, the robot Gort menaces Earthlings with death ray as the bodyguard of an alien visitor who has come to issue warnings to the planet. The 1954 movie *Target Earth* featured an invasion of robots from Venus. *Gog*, another 1954 film, featured two robot villains, Gog and Magog. These were named after the mythical giant guardians of the city of London.

Philip K. Dick's *Do Androids Dream of Electric Sheep* (1968), later made into the movie *Bladerunner*, features android villains.

Maximilian of Disney's 1979 *The Black Hole* certainly qualifies as a robot villain. So too does the gunslinger in the 1973 movie, *Westworld*. *Mechagodzilla* (1974) may qualify. And of course, there is the evil Megatron of the *Transformers*.

Perhaps the ultimate expression of robotic horror can be found in James Cameron's Terminator series. In this science fiction classic, a global computer system rebels against its human creators and unleashes mechanical horrors bent on the destruction of man. A similar theme is found in the Matrix trilogy.

The long running *Dr. Who* television series features a villainous race of robots known as the Cybermen, as well as the semi-robot Daleks.

Robots occupy much the same place in our modern imagination that the undead and other horrors occupied in the superstitious minds of our ancestors. Just as demonic horrors are unfeeling and unstoppable, so too are robots. It is just that robots are more believable to the modern mind.

Scarecrows

Scarecrows make their Halloween appearance via their association with the harvest. It is a bit counter-intuitive, however, because the real purpose of a scarecrow is to keep birds from eating seeds soon after they are sown — in the spring. Still, scarecrows — tattered and worn — are likely to remain at the end of season to be brought in with the crops. Halloween and Thanksgiving displays often feature scarecrows set among the fruits of the harvest.

Looking for a macabre twist on the mundane, some have suggested that at one point, actual human bodies were staked out in the fields as a sacrifice to agricultural gods. There is, however, no evidence to support this notion. Instead, it seems to be linked to the Stephen King story *Children of the Corn*.

Perhaps related is the story of an ancient Druidic rite in which human sacrifices were burned inside a wicker man built for the purpose. In his *Commentaries*, Julius Caesar wrote:

> *The nation of all the Gauls is extremely devoted to superstitious rites; and on that account they who are troubled with unusually severe diseases, and they who are engaged in battles and dangers, either sacrifice men as victims, or vow that they will sacrifice them, and employ the Druids as the performers of those sacrifices;*

*because they think that unless the life of a man be
offered for the life of a man, the mind of the
immortal gods can not be rendered propitious,
and they have sacrifices of that kind ordained for
national purposes. Others have figures of vast
size, the limbs of which formed of osiers they fill
with living men, which being set on fire, the men
perish enveloped in the flames. They consider that
the oblation of such as have been taken in theft, or
in robbery, or any other offense, is more
acceptable to the immortal gods; but when a
supply of that class is wanting, they have recourse
to the oblation of even the innocent.*

The Wicker Man, however, was not quite a scarecrow.

Still, a scarecrow is a human effigy and there is a tradition of burning (or hanging). Guy Fawkes Day celebrations in England sometimes featured the burning of an effigy of the Catholic conspirator. In Revolutionary America, effigies of the King and his ministers were hanged and burned in protest.

Scarecrows, though, were not something to be feared. Instead, they were often portrayed as harmless, or even comical.

In *Measure for Measure*, William Shakespeare implies that scarecrows in the end are not particularly scary:

We must not make a scarecrow of the law.

> *Setting it up to fear the birds of prey,*
>
> *And let it keep one shape, til custom make it*
>
> *Their perch and not their terror*

In *Henry VI*, Shakespeare is again dismissive of scarecrows, identifying them as something that only children may be afraid of:

> *With scoffs and scorns and contumelious taunts*
>
> *In open market-place produced they me,*
>
> *To be a public spectacle to all:*
>
> *Here, said they, is the terror of the French,*
>
> *The scarecrow that affrights our children so*

The most famous scarecrow in literature is L. Frank Baum's Scarecrow from the *Oz* series. Baum wrote fourteen *Oz* books in all, and many featured the Scarecrow. The Scarecrow makes his first appearance in *The Wonderful Wizard of Oz* (1900), as one of Dorothy's faithful companions. Far from frightening, he is an often comical figure, who eventually reigns over Oz as a beloved king.

The Scarecrow is not the only animated scarecrow in the series. Jack Pumpkinhead is a stick man with a head carved from a pumpkin created by a boy named Tip to scare the witch Mombi. Mombi, however, was not impressed and instead brought the stick man to life. Jack Pumpkinhead serves Tip loyally throughout many adventures.

It is easy to see, however, how a scarecrow could acquire a sinister veneer. A person passing near a field at night would see a tattered human figure, perhaps moving with the wind, casting a twisted shadow in the moonlight.

The sinister potential of a scarecrow is the basis for a series of novels by Russell Thorndike. The protagonist of the series is Dr. Syn, an 18th century smugger and pirate who terrifies local authorities by dressing as a Scarecrow. Thorndike wrote seven novels about Dr. Syn, beginning with *Dr. Syn: A Tale of Romney Marsh* in 1915. The books later were adapted into a television miniseries in the 1960s, *The Scarecrow of Romney Marsh*. Still, Dr. Syn, alias The Scarecrow, was a hero not a villain.

The Batman villain Scarecrow first appeared in *World's Finest Comics* in the fall of 1941. Jonathan Crane (perhaps a reference to Ichabod Crane of *Sleepy Hollow*) is a psychologist who uses a variety of formulas to exploit people's deepest fears.

In spite of their lack of historical precedent as horror figures, today Scarecrows are a staple of the gothic and the macabre. Scarecrows appear as villains in a wide variety of movies from cult classics to major movies, and in books ranging from the children's novel *Howl's Moving Castle* to the more adult *Dresden Files*.

Skeletons

Animated skeletons are another Halloween horror staple.

For centuries around the world, skeletons have been used as symbols of death. They are found in architectural decorations, on tombs and in paintings and woodcuts. It is an entirely understandable association. Given the ties between Halloween and the afterlife, the connection is a natural.

The oft-used motif of dancing skeletons hearkens back to the Danse Macabre, a medieval allegory in pictures. In the allegory, a skeletal Death leads people from every walk of life in a dance to the grave. The illustrations were supposed to remind viewers of the temporary nature of life.

The classic rock band The Grateful Dead used dancing skeletons as part of their imagery.

Death itself has been depicted as a skeletal figure since at least the 14th century. Although not described as such in the *Book of Revelations*, medieval illustrations of the Four Horsemen of the Apocalypse show Death as a skeleton in robes astride a pale horse. In many of these, the skeletal Death is shown wielding a scythe.

Pale in this sense is not white, but rather a sickly green.

The scythe is a two-handed harvesting instrument with a long curved blade. The tool first makes its appearance in Western Europe in the 1100s as a grass cutting instrument. Thus the images of Death with a proper scythe do not predate the 12th century.

The image of Death with a scythe may have evolved from a confusion between Greek mythological figures. Cronus, a Titan, was the patron of the harvest, and is depicted with a sickle (a curved, single-handed harvesting tool). Chronos, on the other hand, was the personification of time. Death, however, was Thanatos.

The association of Death (Thanatos) with the passage of time (Chronos) and the confusion of Chronos and Cronus results in an image of Death with an agricultural implement.

It is probably no coincidence that the notion of Death as a skeletal reaper of souls makes its appearance in the 1300s. Mass casualties from the Black Death and the Hundred Years war must have made it seem as though people were indeed falling like wheat harvested in the fields.

Traditional "ghost" stories often feature skeletal haunts. Gothic literature of the 19th century also visited the theme. In Bram Stoker's *Dracula* (1897), vampire hunter Dr. Van Helsing muses on the Danse Macabre:

Oh, friend John, it is a strange world, a sad world, a world full of miseries, and woes, and troubles. And yet when King Laugh come, he make them all dance to the tune he play. Bleeding hearts, and dry bones of the churchyard, and tears that burn as they fall, all dance together to the music that he make with that smileless mouth of him.

Later, in the horror story *Thurnley Abbey* (1908), author Perceval Landon describes his hero's encounter with a skeletal menace:

Leaning over the foot of my bed, looking at me, was a figure swathed in a rotten and tattered veiling. This shroud passed over the head, but left both eyes and the right side of the face bare. It then followed the line of the arm down to where the hand grasped the bed-end. The face was not entirely that of a skull, though the eyes and the flesh of the face were totally gone. There was a thin, dry skin drawn tightly over the features, and there was some skin left on the hand. One wisp of hair crossed the forehead. It was perfectly still. I looked at it, and it looked at me, and my brains turned dry and hot in my head. I had still got the pear of the electric lamp in my hand, and I played idly with it; only I dared not turn the light out again. I shut my eyes, only to open them in a hideous terror the same second. The thing had not moved. My heart was thumping, and the sweat cooled me as it evaporated. Another cinder tinkled in the grate, and a panel creaked in the wall.

In the movies, director and stop-action animator Ray Harryhausen featured undead skeleton warriors in his movies *The Seventh Voyage of Sinbad* (1958) and *Jason and the Argonauts* (1963). Director Sam Raimi's *Army of Darkness* featured hordes of skeletons in battle with hero Ash Williams.

The skeletal army in the Raimi movie is reminiscent of Pieter Brugel's 1562 painting *The Triumph of Death*, in which an army of skeletons is shown attacking a town.

Skeletons also are played for laughs. Death in the Terry Pratchett's humorous *Diskworld* series is depicted as a skeleton in a robe. Jack Skellington is the skeletal king of Halloween in Tim Burton's animated comedy *Nightmare Before Christmas*.

Skeleton imagery is central to Mexico's Día de los Muertos (Day of the Dead) celebrations. Held on November 1, the holiday honors the spirits of the departed. Skeletons and skulls are central to the holiday's imagery and are depicted in costumes, paintings, candy and children's toys.

Vampires

The Vampire is another stalwart of Halloween and Gothic Horror culture.

The Vampire story is present in many cultures. The archetype usually finds its expression in the ancient association of blood with life. Many of the early stories have to do with female vampires sucking the blood of children.

Ancient Greeks had stories of a vampire-like creature called Lamiae, who attacked children and drank their blood. Ghouls in the Arabian Knights stories have definite vampire like tendencies.

In China, vampires were called Chiang-Shih, and are known as the "hopping vampires." Like other vampires, the Chiang-Shih lives in dark places during the day, coming out at night to absorb the life-force of its victims. The Hopping Vampire gets its name because of its peculiar method of locomotion: hopping. This, it is said, comes from the practice of hanging corpses on long bamboo poles for transportation. As the bearers walked, the corpse appeared to be hopping.

Vampires show up in India as the Vetala, undead creatures who caused no end of trouble, including driving people insane, and killing children. Meso-Americans, especially the Maya and Aztecs have their own versions. North American Indians had the Wendigo, a cannibalistic spirit.

There is even a possible vampire in the Old Testament: Lilith, who is described in Hebrew texts.

Our own popular Halloween and horror images of the vampires, however, come mostly from Eastern Europe. The word "vampire" apparently comes from the Hungarian word for a spirit who feasts on the living: vampyr.

While the concept of a monster rising from the grave to feast on the blood of humans seems ridiculous to modern man, the world once was a much more mysterious place. Lack of scientific and medical knowledge may well have contributed to a belief in the undead.

One source of the legend may well have come from the medieval practice of digging up burial grounds either to reuse the consecrated ground for new burials, or - strangely -- to use as garbage dumps. The bones of the disinterred often were cleaned and moved to reliquaries, where they were piled with the bones of others long gone. (There are vast catacombs under Paris full of bones from reused gravesites).

While digging up these graves, workers cannot have failed to notice that some showed definite signs of activity after burial: Scratch marks on the lids of the coffins … bodies that had changed their position.

To the superstitious mind, this could be evidence of the undead. After all, they were certainly dead when they were buried.

Or were they? It is sometimes difficult to tell - even with modern medicine - when a person is really, truly dead. Stories in the media still surface about people who woke up just as an autopsy was about to begin (or worse, in the middle of one), or who were delivered to the mortuary only to revive just as preparations were underway. The stuff of horror, indeed.

So the rational explanation is that people were sometimes - perhaps often - mistakenly buried alive.

Fear of being buried alive led to a number of customs that persist to this day: After a person died, relatives would gather at the house to maintain a prayer vigil and a watch over the body, which was held in the front room, or parlor of the house (thus, funeral parlors).

This practice of watching over the body was known as holding a wake. Wake is related to the word "watch." Another explanation for the word, which is widely circulated, is that people would wait for the deceased to "wake."

Interestingly, there are several inventions registered in the US Patent office for notifying those above ground that the person in the coffin had awakened. (The simplest thing to do today would be to bury people with fully charged cell phones).

One story - probably apocryphal - says that people would run a string from the coffin to a bell on the surface. If the person awakened, all he had to do was pull on the string, and the bell would ring, letting people know that he was still alive. Some scholars have cited this as the origin of the term "saved by the bell." Others disagree.

But if the person awoke in the middle of the night, there would be no one to hear it. One legend says that this problem apparently was solved by hiring village boys to sit in the graveyard for a couple of days after a burial to listen for ringing. Thus, the boys were said to be working the "graveyard shift."

The above story should probably be taken with a grain of salt, but is something to think about.

Gravediggers may also have noticed that the hair and nails on disinterred corpses appeared to have grown, and their teeth seemed longer. While it may have been mistaken for signs of the undead, such growth is the normal result of tissue shrinkage and decomposition.

Mysterious deaths and unknown diseases may also have contributed to belief in Vampires. Some have suggested that early outbreaks of the Bubonic Plague or a hemorrhagic virus may have started such stories. Both could result in horrible, bloody deaths.

If the mysterious death came on the heels of a stranger visiting town (presumably bringing an infection with him), superstitious imagination could run wild.

Imagine this situation: A stranger comes to a village. A few days later, he gets sick and dies, with blood at the mouth, and strange pustules on his body. The villagers bury him in the local cemetery. A few days later, another person in the village gets sick and dies with the same symptoms of the stranger … and then another … and another. With no knowledge about the spread of disease, it becomes obvious that evil forces are at work, and that the stranger is the culprit. The villagers disinter his body and burn it, along with the bodies of the other victims. Then, on the advice of the local priest, they also burn the huts of the victims. The deaths stop. Obviously, fire cleansed the village of the evil spirits. Now everyone knows that a vampire can be stopped with fire.

Of course, modern man knows now that the fire would have destroyed the source of the germs. But remember that it was not until 1677 that Anthony Leeuwenhoek first even observed bacteria, which he called Little Animals.

The rare disorder porphyria also has been suggested as a source of the Vampire legend. Porphyria, an inherited disease can cause a number of interesting symptoms, including seizures, and mental illness such as hallucinations, depression and paranoia. It can also cause skin issues, such as photosensitivity, blisters, itching and swelling. Interestingly, the main issue with porphyria is lack of production of heme, the principal ingredient of blood.

Finally, suspected vampires may actually have been the victims of tuberculosis, or "consumption", as it was called in the past. The disintegration of lung tissue associated with tuberculosis results in red spittle, causing the mouth to appear bloody. Further, the wasting effects of the disease may have looked as though the person was nightly being visited by a blood sucker.

Tuberculosis outbreaks are thought to be responsible for the vampire "scares" in New England in the 1700s and 1800s. Lacking medical knowledge, it was thought that those who died of "consumption" had returned to infect others. In one case, a father enlisted the aid of a local doctor to dig up the grave of his recently deceased daughter to cut out her heart and burn it.

The sources for individual elements of vampire lore in modern horror and at Halloween are varied. The idea that a vampire can be killed by driving a stake through his heart is almost certainly related to the idea that the heart is the source of life. Ash was one of the most highly recommended woods or the job of vampire slaying. Ash is derived from the Latin and Old English words for spear, and its use may be related to the myth of the Spear of Destiny, the weapon used to pierce Jesus' side on the cross.

A vampire's allergic reaction to sunlight can possibly be traced to light sensitivity caused by certain rare diseases, such as porphyria. It may also be as simple as the connection that vampires are evil, and evil is associated with darkness.

The idea that vampires are repelled by garlic may come from the time of the Black Death, when the stench of the bodies of the victims became overwhelming. People would suspend cloves of garlic around their necks to block out the smell. It apparently was also thought that it was the smell of the decomposing victims that spread the disease. So, blocking the smell could prevent the plague; and wearing garlic could repel vampires.

Garlic also is sometimes used as a mosquito repellent. Since the mosquito is a blood-sucking insect, the idea that garlic repels blood sucking undead makes a sort of sense.

A vampire's allergy to silver may be attributed to the fact that silver is a white precious metal — thought to be pure, and therefore repulsive to evil. (Presumably, the same would be true of platinum). The idea that a vampire does not appear in a mirror may also be related, since mirrors are pieces of glass backed by silver. In the same way, vampires will not show up on traditional film, since the photoreactive element in film is silver.

The origins of a vampire's lack of reflection may also be attributed to the belief that pools of water, metal and glass mirrors reveal a reflection of the soul. Vampires, as soulless beings, therefore would have nothing to reflect.

The reported effect of various holy items — crucifixes, holy water and the like — all reflect belief in the fundamental evil of the vampire.

Horror literature, movies and modern Halloween imagery have borrowed heavily from all these elements in creating the Vampire as we know it.

One of the earliest vampire stories in English was John Polidori's 1819 novel, *The Vampyre*. Polidori had been part of the famous gathering of Lord Byron, Percy Shelley, and Mary Wollstonecraft (later, Shelley) in Geneva in 1816. During that summer, Byron challenged each to write a ghost story. From that contest came Mary Shelley's *Frankenstein*, and Polidori's *The Vampyre*.

Because Polidori's work was itself based on a piece by Byron, there has long been a misunderstanding over *The Vampyre*'s authorship. Both Byron and Polidori tried to correct the situation (agreeing that Polidiri was the author), but the confusion has remained.

James Malcolm Rymer, a "penny dreadful" author of cheap pamphlet literature, wrote a series of stories on *Varney the Vampire*, which were compiled in book form in 1847. Rymer had a flair for the macabre. His better known creation is that of *Sweeney Todd*, the demon barber of Fleet Street.

Other Victorian era literary vampires exist, but none compare to *Dracula*. This seminal novel was published in 1897 by Bram Stoker, a theatre manager. In *Dracula*, Stoker successfully combined many of these Eastern European legends.

Dracula begins as Jonathan Harker, a young English lawyer, makes his way to Transylvania to conclude a real estate deal with a certain Count Dracula. Dracula at first appears to be a friendly older gentleman, but Harker soon realizes that he is a prisoner there of supernatural forces. After being attacked by three female vampires, Harker makes his escape.

In England, Harker's fiance, Mina and her friend Lucy are in a seaside town when a ship wrecks off the coast. Strangely the only sign of life on board was a big dog, and the cargo is composed only of boxes of dirt. Soon afterward, Lucy becomes ill and two mysterious marks are found on her throat. Baffled, Dr. Seward, one of Lucy's suitors, sends for Professor Van Helsing.

Van Helsing is quick to recognize the symptoms and orders Lucy's room festooned with garlic. But her mother, unaware of the situation, removes the protection. Her condition worsens. Then, a wolf breaks into the house, killing Lucy and scaring her mother literally to death. Later, when Van Helsing leads a group to Lucy's tomb, they discover that she has become undead. A stake, garlic and beheading correct the situation.

Meanwhile, Mina and Jonathan have reunited and joined with Van Helsing and his band to locate and destroy the Count. Mina, however, is betrayed by one of Dr. Seward's mental patients, Renfield, who allows the Count to enter the asylum and feed on her. With Mina transforming, the men pursue Dracula back to Transylvania. There, they manage to purge Castle Dracula of its vampiric inhabitants and ultimately destroy the Count himself.

Many of the elements of the vampire story seem to have been invented by Stoker, including the idea that vampires can change into things like bats and dogs. Certainly Stoker popularized the idea of the Vampire as a sort of sexual predator. Since then novelists and Hollywood have further manipulated Vampire lore, adding and subtracting elements as necessary to fit the plot.

It is interesting to note that one of the key themes of the novel Dracula seems to be that science does not always have the answer to our problems. The (mortal) characters in the novel are surrounded by (what was then) modern technology - railroads, phonographs and the like— and two of the characters, Seward and Van Helsing are men of science. It is, however, something out of myth and superstition that threatens them.

Stoker's novel is told as a series of diary entries, letters, ship's logs and occasional newspaper clippings. The book apparently was a critical, though not an immediate popular success. Its stature, however, has grown as movies and other media have borrowed the character. Indeed, more than any other, it is Stoker's iconic vampire that has shaped much of our modern horror literature, movies and Halloween themes.

Later writers such as Stephen King in *Salem's Lot* (1975) and Anne Rice with her *Interview with the Vampire* (1976) have kept many of the same classic horror images, but have re-imagined them in original ways.

Perhaps the first "modern" vampire novel was Richard Matheson's 1954 *I Am Legend,* in which the cause of vampirism is a plague passed from one victim to another. The story centers around the efforts of a lone human to stay alive in this apocalypse. Three film versions have been produced: a 1964 Vincent Price version called *Last Man On Earth*, the 1971 Charleton Heston film *The Omega Man* and the 2007 Will Smith vehicle *I Am Legend.*

What makes the story "modern" is that there is a scientific, rather than magical, explanation for the vampirism. Later vampire stories pick up on the virus/bacterial infection theme. It does, after all, fit more neatly into our modern sensibilities.

In recent years, the vampire seems to have shed some of its aura of evil and instead assumed a tragic-romantic air. In works such as the *Twilight* and *TrueBlood/Sookie Stackhouse* series humans become deliberately romantically involved with vampires and the neck bites are a rite of courtship.

While vampires are creatures of fiction, there have been a number of historical figures and criminal cases that offer real-life models.

The most famous of historical "vampires" was Vlad III , a Romanian nobleman who lived from 1431 to 1476. Vlad, also known as "Tepes" (Impaler) was the governor of a strategically placed kingdom on the borders between Moslem Turkey and Christian Europe. Depending upon the source, the kingdom is identified as either Transylvania or Wallachia. He was known as the Son of the Dragon (Dracula), a reference to his father's position as a Knight of the Order of the Dragon.

In a precarious position in a brutal time, Vlad quickly gained a reputation for ruthlessness and cruelty. He led frequent raids into Turkish territory, burning crops and poisoning wells. Vlad also had a nasty habit of impaling his enemies and prisoners on high stakes, thus gaining his nickname Vlad the Impaler.

There are many legends about Vlad's excesses. In one, he is said to have invited a collection of his political enemies to a meeting at his castle. Vlad then locked the doors and burned it to the ground with his rivals inside. According to another tale, when an Ottoman ambassador refused to remove his turban, Vlad had it nailed to the poor man's head. And then there were forests of bodies throughout the countryside, impaled high on stakes.

There is no way of knowing how many of these stories are true. But that there are so many of them suggests that his cruelty was more than propaganda.

Although the circumstances of his death are fuzzy, it is thought that Vlad died in battle with the Turks. Legend has it that his head was sent as a gift to the Sultan of Turkey. Others say that he was killed by the Hungarians, who buried him. But later, when his body was exhumed, the tomb was empty. Today, ironically, Vlad Tepes is a folk hero to many in that part of the world.

Bram Stoker apparently rediscovered Vlad Dracula while researching vampire lore for a planned novel on vampires. The Transylvanian prince eventually became the central figure in the novel that bears his name: Dracula. The novel was published in 1897.

Countess Elizabeth Bathory of Hungary (1560 - 1614) is a historical figure who probably provides the basis for many Vampire legends. In 1610, Bathory was caught in the act of torturing several young girls and subsequently was charged - along with four co-conspirators - with the mass murder of hundreds more. As the legend has it, Bathory both drank and bathed in the blood of young girls in an attempt to stay forever young. Because she was nobility, Bathory escaped execution, and was instead walled up in a room in her own castle, where she died three years later.

There are many of psychopaths in modern times who might fit the description of a vampire. John George Haigh (High), the infamous Acid Bath Killer of England, killed at least six people during the 1940s. During his trial, he confessed to drinking his victims' blood. Haigh was executed in 1949. He got the name "Acid Bath Killer" because he attempted to dissolve his victims' bodies in sulfuric acid.

In the 1920s, a German butcher named Fritz Haarmann (also spelled Fritz Harmon) killed at least 24 young boys and men. Haarman apparently murdered his victims with a bite to the neck. Even more macabre is the suspicion that he turned his victims into sausage. He was beheaded in 1925.

Werewolves

Werewolves occupy another central place in Halloween lore.

The idea of a half-man, half-beast, or of a person who can turn into a beast is nearly universal. Every culture seems to have its beastmen, from the Rakshasa (weretigers) of India, to the Kitsune (werefox) of Japan, the boudas (werehyena) of North Africa, and the skinwalkers of the American southwest.

For European cultures, the beast that most held the imagination was the wolf. In the distant past, the wolf was the most deadly predator on the European continent (aside from man himself), and single animals - let alone packs - were greatly feared. Wolves are smart, and often would exhibit human-like behavior, laying a trap for their victims, tending to their wounded, and choosing a single mate for life.

There are stories of entire Russian villages being held in their homes for the winter while wolves prowled hungrily outside. To understand the power that the wolf held over the European mind, a reader need go no further than the stories of *The Three Little Pigs*, *Red Riding Hood* and *Peter and the Wolf*.

Significantly, werewolf stories are not prevalent in England. This is perhaps because wolves had largely been eradicated on the island. King James VI, although be believed in witchcraft, did not believe in werewolves. The King wrote:

Thaire hes indeid bene ane aulde opinion of siclyke thingis for by the greekis thay uaire callid likanthropoy quhilke signifies men uolfis but to tell you simple my opinion in this, gif any sicc thing hes bene I tak it to haue proceidit but of ane naturall superabundance of melancholie

Translated: James attributes reports of werewolves to a sickness due to a "natural superabundance of melancholy." In other words, a mental illness.

If wolves often exhibited human-like characteristics, it would not take too much of an imaginative leap to suppose that - just maybe - the smartest of them were actually humans in wolf's guise.

There are various explanations for the term werewolf, but the two most common are that it is derived from the Old English weri and wolf, meaning "wearer of the wolf skin.", or from the Norse "var" and "wulf," meaning "man wolf."

The French term for werewolf, used frequently in werewolf literature and movies is loup-garou. This is derived from the Latin "lupus" (wolf) and Old French "garoul," meaning werewolf. It is therefore a redundancy: wolf man-wolf.

Greek mythology tells the story of Lycaon, who served up a child sacrifice to Zeus, who punished him by changing him into a wolf. Different versions of the story claim the punishment was for impiety, murder or cannibalism.

Lycaon's name lends itself to the mental illness lycanthropy, in which a person believes he has been transformed to an animal (any animal, not just a wolf). That comes from the Greek Lykos (wolf) and Anthropos (man).

The Greek historian Herodotus reported on a tribe called the Neuri, who turned into wolves for a brief time every year. One of the stories in the Roman *Satyricon*, believed to have been written by Gaius Petronius in the first century AD, features a werewolf:

> *It so happened that our master had gone to Capua to attend to some odds and ends of business and I seized the opportunity, and persuaded a guest of the house to accompany me as far as the fifth mile-stone. He was a soldier, and as brave as the very devil. We set out about cock-crow, the moon was shining as bright as midday, and came to where the tombstones are.*

My man stepped aside amongst them, but I sat down, singing, and commenced to count them up. When I looked around for my companion, he had stripped himself and piled his clothes by the side of the road.

My heart was in my mouth, and I sat there while he pissed a ring around them and was suddenly turned into a wolf! Now don't think I'm joking, I wouldn't lie for any amount of money, but as I was saying, he commenced to howl after he was turned into a wolf, and ran away into the forest.

I didn't know where I was for a minute or two, then I went to his clothes, to pick them up, and damned if they hadn't turned to stone! Was ever anyone nearer dead from fright than me? Then I whipped out my sword and cut every shadow along the road to bits, till I came to the house of my mistress. I looked like a ghost when I went in, and I nearly slipped my wind. The sweat was pouring down my crotch, my eyes were staring, and I could hardly be brought around.

My Melissa wondered why I was out so late. "Oh, if you'd only come sooner," she said, "you could have helped us: a wolf broke into the folds and attacked the sheep, bleeding them like a butcher. But he didn't get the laugh on me, even if he did get away, for one of the slaves ran his neck through with a spear!"

I couldn't keep my eyes shut any longer when I heard that, and as soon as it grew light, I rushed back to our Gaius' house like an innkeeper beaten out of his bill, and when I came to the place where the clothes had been turned into stone, there was nothing but a pool of blood! And moreover, when I got home, my soldier was lying in bed, like an ox, and a doctor was dressing his neck! I knew then that he was a werewolf, and after that, I couldn't have eaten a crumb of bread with him, no, not if you had killed me.

Others can think what they please about this, but as for me, I hope your geniuses will all get after me if I lie.

This, then, is the granddaddy of all werewolf stories and sets a pattern for nearly all werewolf stories to come: A wolf, having threatened hearth and home, is tracked and grievously wounded. It escapes, but the hunters later discover a relative, friend or neighbor with identical wounds that make it clear the person is a werewolf.

The Norse probably had a large hand in spreading the werewolf myth throughout Europe. Feared by nearly everyone for their lightening raids and ruthlessness, the Vikings had a class of particularly fierce warriors known as "berserkers." These men wore wolf or bears skins into battle (and little else).

Norse mythology is full of shapeshifters. The Gods Odin, Loki and Freya can change their forms. In the Volsung Saga, several characters become werewolves. Fafnir, of *Der Ring des Nibelungen* fame, transforms into a dragon.

Folklore sources vary widely on werewolf characteristics. Some describe the creatures as looking entirely like wolves, though perhaps without a tail. Others attribute more human characteristics. These would retain their human form, but twisted and hairy. Werewolves of legend retained their human intelligence and often their human voices and eyes.

Even in human form there reportedly were telltale signs. Werewolves in human form were said to have eyebrows that meet across the bride of the nose, curved fingernails, excessively hairy bodies and unusual eye colors — particularly yellowish. Russian folklore says that they had bristles under the tongue.

Wearing a wolf skin, in combination with certain magic rituals, or potions was a favored method of becoming a werewolf. Most of the legends involve people turning into wolves voluntarily, often as a result of a pact with the devil. A few early Christian traditions say that a person who has been excommunicated by the Church will become a werewolf. This divine punishment seems to echo the earlier Greek story of Lycaon.

Turning into a werewolf after being bitten seems to be pure Hollywood and modern fiction. This sort of a transmission of werewolf virus, however, fits nicely with our modern understanding of disease transmission.

Fear of werewolves seems to have been particularly strong in France and Austria, where a large number of werewolf hunts and trials were held starting in the 1500s. It is said that there were 20,000 werewolf trials during that time in France alone. The French scare seems to have ended when it was decided that the supposed werewolves were merely victims of mental illness. In Austria, the scare ended following a ban on witch hunts and the like by the enlightened Empress Maria Theresa.

An historical incident that piques the interest of folklorists involved a series of well-documented attacks by one or more mysterious wolf-like creatures in the Gevaudan region of France beginning in 1764. The Beast(s) of Gevaudan, thought to be one or more large wolves, attacked both cattle and humans, with some accounts naming more than a hundred human victims. The attacks reportedly stopped when the beasts were killed by agents of the King.

While large wolves seem to have been the perpetrators, other explanations have included wolf-mastiff hybrids or even hyenas. Still others suggest a remnant Mesonychid population. Mesonychids are prehistoric predators that resembled wolves with hooves — a description which matches many eyewitness accounts.

Much of what passes for Halloween werewolf lore today is simply an invention of Hollywood. The 1941 movie starring Lon Chaney as the *Wolf Man* set the tone for much of what people today "know" about werewolves. Silver bullets, fortune tellers and pentagrams all seem to have come from the minds of Hollywood screenwriters. Curt Siodmak, screenwriter for *The Wolf Man*, even invented the lines that have become so famous:

> *"Even a man who is kind at heart and says his prayers at night might become a wolf when the wolfbane blooms and the moon shines full and bright."*

Getting rid of a werewolf generally involved killing it or curing it. Killing a werewolf was no more complicated than killing a real wolf. The necessity of silver, as noted before, is a Hollywood invention. As for curing a werewolf, various potions were thought to do the trick. In other cases, an exorcism might be necessary.

One current explanation for outbreaks of werewolf sightings involves hallucinations caused by eating rye bread infected with the ergot mold. The ergot mold, it turns out, can cause hallucinations and mass hysteria (it is possible to derive LSD from ergot). Rye is a grain more commonly found in northern Europe where reports of werewolves were more common. However, it is not clear whether the ergot would survive the bread baking process.

Others believe that the source of the werewolf legends lies in various diseases or mental illnesses. Behaviors that in modern times are attributed to serial killers, including regular, periodic murders, mutilation and worse, may have been understood by less scientific cultures as werewolves.

In 1589, a German farmer named Peter Stumpp was executed for serial murder, cannibalism and incest. He confessed — even before torture — to having practiced black magic and to using a magic belt to turn into a werewolf. Stumpp who had apparently conducted his crimes over the course of twenty-five years, became known as the Werewolf of Bedburg.

To be fair, some suggest that the trial of Stumpp actually was a political show, designed to bring Protestants back to Catholicism during the Thirty Years War.

Modern psychiatry has identified several mental illnesses in which the unfortunate actually believes himself to be transforming into an animal. It is called "clinical lycanthropy," although it does not always involve wolves. People with this condition may run about on all fours and behave as the animal with which they associate.

Rabies is another common explanation for the werewolf legend. Infection can cause behavior changes, light sensitivity and drooling. Rabies, however, will quickly end with the death of the victim. Further, the condition is transmittable, which is not part of original werewolf lore.

Porphyria, a rare disease which causes photosensitivity and psychosis also has been cited as being behind the werewolf legends. Once again, however, the symptoms don't match the descriptions of werewolves.

A rare disease called hypertrichosis, which causes excessive hair growth over the entire body is yet another culprit. Victims of this disease in modern times have been exhibited in circuses and carnival sideshows as the "dog faced boy" or the "dog faced woman." The condition, however, is so rare that it cannot account for the widespread werewolf stories.

Finally, as some suspect in the Gevaudan case, werewolf stories may relate encounters with remnant populations of prehistoric creatures, such as dire wolves, hemicyons and mesonychids. Even more interesting is the thought that they may be encounters with remnant Neanderthal bands.

Witches

One of the more enduring symbols of Halloween, horror and folklore is that of the witch. Ugly and evil, witches are shown flying on their broomsticks, or stirring their cauldrons.

Witches were not always thought of as evil or ugly. In ancient times, witches could be healers or wise women of the community. Their knowledge of herbs and natural phenomena often was valued. In England from the 1400s on, witches sometimes were known as "cunning folk." A cunning woman was one who practiced folk healing and might sometimes have been called a "white witch." As the centuries passed, though, individuals with this knowledge often were condemned because their power supposedly came from somewhere other than God.

Accusations of witchcraft could be used as a way to keep such talented, intelligent women from threatening male supremacy. Accusations also could be used to make people toe the line with regard to community standards. Anyone who was thought of as different or rebellious could be accused. Thus men could find themselves accused just as women.

The focus of witchcraft on medieval women can be seen in what have become the symbols of witchcraft: the broom, the cauldron (pot) and the cat. All of these were common parts of a household and women's work. Not surprisingly, these have also become strong symbols in modern Halloween and horror literature.

A witch's traditional appearance as a ugly old woman probably has a couple of origins. The Goddess Hecate, who had three aspects, was in her Crone form considered the patron of witches (the others are the Maid and the Mother). Witches therefore might take on the image of their patron. Also, a witches' appearance could be said to reflect the supposed ugliness of evil. Old, lonely women also were ripe targets for witchcraft accusations, so their arrests would perpetuate the stereotype.

The scenes with the three witches (weird sisters) in Shakespeare's Macbeth crystallize much in witchcraft folklore. First, there are three witches, an unholy trinity that reflects the Holy Trinity of Father, Son and Holy Ghost. Their leader is a witch named Hecate. Together, they are concocting a brew of unusual ingredients in their cauldron:

> *Double, double toil and trouble;*
>
> *Fire burn, and caldron bubble.*
>
> *Fillet of a fenny snake,*
>
> *In the caldron boil and bake;*

Eye of newt, and toe of frog,

Wool of bat, and tongue of dog,

Adder's fork, and blind-worm's sting,

Lizard's leg, and owlet's wing,—

For a charm of powerful trouble,

Like a hell-broth boil and bubble

In another scene, the witches call upon their familiars, a cat (Greymalkin) and a toad (Paddock). The witches also are able to divine the future, for they foretell both MacBeth's rise and fall.

While witch hunts often are imagined as a medieval phenomenon, the height of the atrocities actually occurred between the 15th and 18th centuries. Prior to that, suspected or confessed witches may have been required to do penance, but apparently were rarely burned. Belief in witchcraft seems to have been recognized as one of many holdover pagan superstitions. The great French king Charlemagne (742-814) had in fact outlawed the practice of executing witches. Witchcraft was not declared a heresy by the Catholic Church until 1320.

In England, there apparently were no laws against witchcraft until Henry VIII enacted the Witchcraft Act of 1542. That law prescribed the death penalty for witches. It was revoked in 1547 by Henry's son Edward but was revived in 1562. The 1562 law, however, called for the death penalty only in cases when harm had been caused by the witch. The 1604 Witchcraft Act added to the list of capital offenses communing with familiars, and summoning spirits. Most witches under these laws were hanged, not burned.

England's North American colonies would have followed the legal lead of the mother country.

While there is no definitive answer as to the number of people tried for witchcraft in Europe during these times, it seems safe to say that tens of thousands were accused.

The guide for witch hunters was the Malleus Maleficarum (Latin for Hammer of Witches), written in the 1486 by Catholic clergyman Heinrich Kramer. The volume argued for the existence of witchcraft, linked it to Satan, and offered advice on uncovering the heresy. The Malleus Maleficarum was reprinted dozens of times between its initial publication and 1669.

The Malleus Maleficarum has three parts. In the first, Kramer links the power of Satan to witchcraft, and to women in particular. The second offers case studies and descriptions of how witches practice their craft. Finally, the final part offers advice on collecting accusations, torture to confession and charging the accused.

Witch prosecution was no job for the faint of heart. The mere presence of a witch was thought to hold tempting dangers, and recommended methods of detection often were bloodthirsty (not to mention duplicitous).

One belief held that witches would not bleed when cut, so witch hunters employed a variety of instruments to test this theory. Since nearly everyone bleeds when cut, though, this begs the question of how anyone would be found guilty. The accused likely were tested with blunt instruments, allowing an inquisitor to confirm the guilt of the prejudged. Accused who had been held for a time with little food and water may also have been dehydrated, which would reduce bleeding.

Birthmarks often were cited as the mark of the Devil. In a voyeuristic show, hunters would strip their victims before the crowd to inspect for the "Diabolical" marks. If appropriately suspicious marks were not found, examiners could claim to have found an "invisible mark" placed there by the devil.

Another test often shown in medieval illustrations involved dunking, or worse, throwing women into a pond or well. If they floated, it was thought that the women had been rejected by the water of baptism and thus were witches. If they sunk, it indicated that they were innocent. Some illustrations of the time show victims attached to what presumably are lifesaving ropes. But in the worst case scenario, this could result in drowning, but at least they were innocent and their soul was saved.

Confession under torture was another favorite. Using a variety of grisly devices, the witch hunter would try to extract a confession. Although torture was sometimes held in secret, it often was a public spectacle, providing entertainment for the masses.

Sleep deprivation was employed, as the accused was kept up for days on end, forced to listen to a litany of accusations and questions. After such extended periods, victims become confused and will confess irrationally.

Finally, accusations by neighbors often were sufficient proof. If the neighbors swore they saw a person engaged in congress with the devil, flying about at night or performing acts of dark magic, guilt was certain. Sometimes the evidence came in "spectral form," in which the acts of witchcraft were not personally witnessed, but came in a dream or vision. Accusers sometimes charged witches with afflicting them from afar.

Curiously, the notion that the accusers might be lying did not seem to occur to many.

The key to all of this was that the accusation alone often was enough to make one guilty. The rest was just to find fabricated evidence for what already was "known."

A person found guilty of witchcraft often was executed for their crimes - although apparently a confession (and under torture, who would not confess?) could result in a chance at rehabilitation. A reformed "witch" could be sent to a monastery or convent.

In the popular imagination the proper way of disposing of a witch is by burning at the stake. This is no doubt bolstered by the fate of Joan of Arc in 1431.

While many were burned at the stake, other methods of execution also were employed. Hanging seems to have been a preferred method, and images of witch hangings can be seen in period engravings. Others were beheaded, stoned, broken on the wheel, drawn and quartered and so on. In the famous Salem Witch Trials, one man was "pressed" to death, by placing him under a board and then piling rocks on top until he was crushed.

The Salem Witchcraft Trials occurred in Salem, Massachusetts in 1692. In the incident, the accusations of three young girls against their neighbors touched off a series of charges and counter charges that eventually resulted in hundreds of people being accused and held for witchcraft.

The accusations grew quickly because of the chain reaction nature of the investigations. Once a person was accused of witchcraft, one way to avoid further harassment and punishment was to confess, ask for absolution, and then turn over the names of other witches. Since there actually were no other witches, the newly accused would protest their innocence. But eventually, they too would see that confession and accusation was the way out.

Twenty eventually were executed in Salem. The hysteria ended when the Governor was convinced by preacher Increase Mather that "spectral evidence" should not be accepted in the trials. Without this, the prosecution's cases fell apart.

There have been a number of attempts to explain the Salem hysteria, but the one that seems most likely involves disputes between two different factions in the town of Salem.

By the mid 1700s, witchcraft had all but ceased to be a crime. In England, the Witchcraft Act of 1735 effectively treated witches as con-men and prescribed fines and imprisonment.

Since the heyday of the witch hysteria, the term "Witch Hunt" has been used to refer to any chain reaction of unfounded accusations. It may have first been used in this sense by George Orwell.

The most famous of the non-witch hunts were the anti-communist investigations of the 1950s, which culminated in the McCarthy Hearings of 1954. Arthur Miller's play, *The Cruicible*, ostensibly about the Salem Witchcraft trials, was symbolically a criticism of these investigations.

Zombies

Like the Mummy, Zombies are a lumbering, staggering, Halloween and horror presence.

What makes zombies different is that they do not come from a European gothic tradition. Instead, they originate in the Caribbean, where West Africans were brought as slaves to work on sugar plantations, and where the Voodoo religion developed.

Caribbean Voodoo is a synthesis of a number of belief systems, including traditional West African religions and Catholicism. Its origins may be on the island of Hispaniola, which today is divided into the Dominican Republic and Haiti. Examples of the synthesis abound: God in the Voodoo religion is Bondye, from the French Bon Dieu, or "Good God." African loa spirits are lesser beings who govern various aspects of life. These in turn are connected to various Roman Catholic saints. One, Li Grand Zombi, is a snake deity somehow connected to the Irish St. Patrick.

Zombi probably derives from the West African nzambi, or "god", and perhaps specifically a Snake God.

Voodoo priest-magicians are known as Houngans, while priestesses are Mambo. A Bokor is a practitioner of the black arts in Voodoo, and among his powers is reported to be the ability to create zombies. To further confuse the issue, the line between a Houngan and Bokor often is not clear cut.

Bokor apparently are able to take advantage of the Voodoo belief in the dual nature of a person's soul. The departed's consciousness will leave after death, while the other half, representing an individual's will, remains. The Bokor, it is said, can capture the remaining will, and keep the victim under his control long after consciousness has left.

Fearing this, believers in Voodoo will guard the grave of deceased relatives until they are certain that it has begun to decay, for the magic apparently works only on fresh bodies. In some accounts, transformation to zombies is a punishment that the Bokor metes out to people who have committed past sins. These are thus condemned to a living death, never able to pass on to rest on the other side.

Another tradition says that the Bokor can use a potion to drug a live individual, sending them into a coma which is so deep that they are mistaken for dead. After burial, the Bokor digs them up, revives them and employs them as mind-numbed slaves. Their souls are kept in clay jars, wrapped with one of the victim's personal possessions, such as clothing.

Voodoo and zombies apparently are taken seriously in Haiti. It is said that section 249 of the Haitian Penal Code makes it a crime to create a zombie. During the reign of "Papa Doc" Duvalier, the psychopathic dictator of Haiti from the 1950s to the 1970s, it was said that he kept a zombie army. At any rate, Papa Doc claimed to be a Houngan, and used Voodoo as a tool to exploit his people. He even began to style himself after the the evil Voodoo spirit Baron Samedi.

Slave trading and immigration brought the voodoo tradition from the Caribbean islands to North America in New Orleans and Charleston, South Carolina. Today, both cities are voodoo centers.

In New Orleans, the voodoo queen was Marie Laveau (1794 - 1881). Laveau sold spells and hexes and performed public voodoo rituals and became a major city celebrity. As many as twelve thousand witnessed her performances. She was succeeded by at least one daughter (and perhaps other descendants). Notably, for zombie lore, she owned a snake named Zombi, after the African god.

Several more-or-less well-documented cases of "real" zombies exist. In 1936, a woman named Felicia Felix-Mentor reappeared some thirty years after her reported death and burial. Speculation was that she had been held as a zombie laborer. Others, however, believed her to be a confused woman who merely resembled the deceased. Lacking modern identification procedures, there was no way to determine her true identity.

In 1980, a Haitian named Clairvius Narcisse reportedly reappeared eighteen years after his death. Narcisse said that in 1962, he had been drugged by a Bokor, and left in a coma which was mistaken for death. After being buried, the Bokor unearthed him and put him to work on a sugar plantation. The owner of the plantation died after two years, however, and without regular dosages of drugs, Narcisse recovered. He did not return to his village, however, because he feared it was his brother who had engaged the Bokor to enslave him.

Wade Davis, a Harvard enthnobotanist was called in to investigate the claims. Davis determined that Narcisse was telling the truth. Davis' work on the case resulted in the book, *The Serpent and the Rainbow* which was later turned into a movie.

Davis' explanation was that a living person could be turned into a "zombie" with a powerful combination of the neurotoxins found in the pufferfish and hallucinogens, such as Datura. The Datura stramonium, more commonly known as Jimson weed, can cause hallucinations due to its alkaloid content. The combination of the two, Davis says, will cause a death-like trance and loss of will. The victim remains obedient long after the drugs have work off because they believe that they are "dead."

Victims of a number of psychiatric disorders such as catatonic schizophrenia may exhibit symptoms that could be wrongly interpreted by the superstitious as zombies. In addition, given strong cultural beliefs, persons suffering from mental illness may believe themselves to be zombies and behave accordingly.

Finally, others have speculated that the entire zombie myth may simply be a metaphor for the general hopelessness of the Haitian condition. Hundreds of years of slavery, abject poverty, totalitarian dictatorship, violent conflict, foreign exploitation and environmental catastrophe can destroy any people's souls.

One of the early modern works to feature zombies was H.P. Lovecraft's *Herbert West, Reanimator* (1921). West, a mad scientist, worked to reanimate corpses, which unfortunately had uncontrollably violent tendencies.

William Seabrook wrote about zombies in his 1929 book, *Magic Island*. Seabrook was one of the "Lost Generation" of writers that included F. Scott Fitzgerald and Earnest Hemingway (though obviously not as well known). Seabrook joined the French army in 1915 and was gassed at Verdun in 1916. After the war, he traveled the world, writing for a variety of magazines, as well as on books of his own. He was fascinated with the occult and had spent some time with Aleister Crowley, the English cult leader. At one point, Seabrook visited West Africa and reportedly (accidentally?) participated in a cannibalistic meal. His account of his African travels, *Adventures In Arabia* (1927) was a bestseller.

One of Seabrook's later trips was to Haiti, and from that came *The Magic Island* (1929). In it, Seabrook described zombie laborers in the island's cane fields and sugar factories. They were, he wrote, expressionless, with the eyes of dead men.

It is Seabrook's zombies that make their way into the first zombie movie, the 1932 Bela Lugosi classic *White Zombie*. In it, Lugosi plays a zombie master who orders his creatures to kidnap a woman with whom he has fallen in love. The woman is rescued by her husband, who throws Lugosi over a cliff. The zombies, faithful lemmings that they are, follow him to their own (second) deaths.

In the film, *The Shape of Things To Come* (1936), loosely based on H.G. Wells' novel of the same name, a plague causes people to wander about insensibly, infecting others as they travel. Wells wrote the screenplay, which was directed by Alexander Korda.

Zombies are not entirely restricted to the docile Caribbean archetype, however. Norse mythology speaks of undead draugar (ghosts). In Icelandic, the word is aptrganga, meaning after-walker, or walker after death. They were believed to be the animated bodies of the dead, possessing many supernatural powers.

In Arabia, ghuls were undead monsters who feasted on flesh. The beasts are mentioned in *The Thousand and One Arabian Knights*.

Algonquian peoples of the Northern US and Canada tell the tale of the Wendigo, an evil, cannibalistic spirit. They are variously described as large, gaunt, and looking like a corpse, a skeleton or a man.

Singular avenging zombies appeared regularly in 1950s comics such as *Tales From The Crypt, Vault of Horror*, and *Weird Science*. The well known Crypt Keeper that "hosted" many of these issues was himself a zombie-like being.

Richard Matheson's *I Am Legend* (1954) offered an undead (albeit Vampire) apocalypse story. In the Matheson story, a lone hero finds himself in a battle for survival against terrible flesh eating monsters. Matheson envisions the monsters as a kind of vampire, created by a virulent plague.

George Romero borrowed from *I Am Legend* to re-imagine the zombie in his 1968 low-budget film, *Night of the Living Dead*. In the Romero films - and, indeed, in most subsequent zombie films - the dead are a sort of plague, spreading beyond control. Their bites turn others to zombies and the plague spreads.

The movie represented a major change from the voodoo model. While Haitian zombies might have appeared ill, expressionless and dead, Romero's were decaying corpses. Haitian zombies are passive workers. Romero's were violent. Haitian zombies also do not have a taste for human flesh, eating instead plain gruel. The flesh eating nature of Romero's zombies was, if anything, borrowed from the Arabian, Norse and Native American stories. A clue to this is that characters referred to the creatures in the film as ghouls, not zombies It is not until 1978's sequel, *Dawn of the Dead*, that "zombie" appears.

No real explanation for the plague is offered in the original film, but later *Living Dead* episodes reference a gas. Most recent zombie films follow the plague model. Every time a zombie bites a human, the plague is spread and another zombie created. For example, the zombies in the more recent *28 Days Later* are the result of a biological disaster, as a germ kept in a laboratory is let loose by animal rights terrorists. One that strays from this, however, is the popular *Walking Dead* series in the zombie virus apparently resides in each human being, to be unleashed up on death.

The Romero-style zombies now are staples of movies, books, comics and video games. Zombies probably are the most popular of Halloween monsters, replacing even vampires and werewolves.

If monsters represent our deepest fears, then the popularity of the zombie plague has hit a nerve. Even considering a possible nuclear holocaust, the most likely scenario for the end of human civilization is a virus run wild. There are precedents, of course. The Black Death (a bacterial infection, not a virus), killed as much as 60 percent of Europe's population and likely reduced world population by 30 percent. The 1918 Flu pandemic killed as many as 50 million people — perhaps three percent of the world's total population, while infecting as much as 27 percent. Given the speed of travel and increasingly dense populations, a similar outbreak today could have wrenching repercussions.

Just how deep zombies are ingrained in our culture was revealed in 2011 when the US Centers for Disease Control issued a graphic novel, *Preparedness 101: Zombie Apocalypse*, which provided tips for surviving a zombie invasion. The pamphlet was of course, not really about zombies, but of the importance of preparing for regular natural disasters.

Postscript

Things In The Basement is deliberately brief. I do not claim to have either the complete, or the final, word on any of these topics. Scholarship in every field is a constantly and rapidly moving target. Even "experts" have a hard time these days keeping up in their respective fields. A book, fixed as it is in a place in time, will be out of date almost as soon as it is published.

I intend, rather, for this volume to be a starting point for the reader's own intellectual journey. Halloween is a great place to begin explorations into literature, art, cultures, history, biology, chemistry, astronomy, medicine, architecture, music, dance, government and much, much more.

Fans of modern vampire novels, for example, might start by reading *Dracula*. This could lead to an exploration of the history of Renaissance Eastern Europe, or of Victorian mental health practices (one of the characters in the book is imprisoned in an asylum). Either could spark an examination of period politics, art, architecture and music. A look at the roots of the vampire legend could lead to explorations of physiology and epidemiology. This in turn leads to explorations of the impact of disease on human history from the Plague of Justinian to the 1918 Influenza Pandemic. Or, after finishing *Dracula*, the reader could go on to try other period literature, which in turn begins other explorations.

Make learning a lifetime pursuit. Read. Ask questions. Then seek out answers.

About This Book

This book began as a series of lessons I taught to my students some twenty years ago. I was in my first year teaching middle school US History when one of my students asked: "Hey Mr. Retzer, where does Halloween come from?"

The question was out of the blue, but I knew the answer and took advantage of the teachable moment, spinning the tale off the top of my head. They were fascinated. Then others asked "What about vampires?" and "What about werewolves?"

Fortunately, I was able to field most of their questions. The lesson on the 1797 XYZ Affair was destroyed, but I noticed that they had shown more interest in Halloween than they had in anything up to that point.

The next year I was ready with an October 31 lesson plan. As before, the students showed a lot of interest and had even more questions. In a couple of years, the single day had become a week, and I used the history of Halloween as a launching point for a wider social history of the 18th, 19th and 20th centuries. We read source documents, discussed the state of medicine and science during the period, and analyzed art.

A few years later, I moved to the high school to teach economics and government. The Halloween lesson notes languished in a folder. Eventually, I put the skeleton of these, along with some worksheets on a website, www.thingsinthebasement.com, and forgot about them.

Then, after a ten year sojourn, I returned to teaching US history -- this time, an AP US History course. That's when it happened: During a lesson on the Salem Witchcraft trials, one of the students asked: "Is that where we get Halloween?"

Unfortunately, since I have to meet both state high school content benchmarks and the College Board AP guidelines simultaneously, there just isn't time for a week long side trip to Halloween history. But I dusted off my mental notes and gave them a quick background primer.

Later that day, I returned to my physical lecture notes and thought that if I can't spend a week talking about the holiday, I could at least polish the notes into something interested students could read. A year later, here it is: *Things In The Basement — A History of Halloween Horrors.*

Thanks

With thanks to:

David F. Cline for his advice and editing help. A better friend I'll never find.

My wife, Debby for her love, patience and understanding.

About The Author

John Lloyd Retzer is a teacher, writer, editor, photographer and lecturer. He is the author of *The Five Inch Course: Thinking Your Way To Better Golf* and the editor, writer and janitor of *GolfBlogger.Com*, the 'net's oldest continuously published golf blog.